FOLENS ENGLISH

PERCEPTIONS

TERRY BROWN
MIKE FLEMING

Perceptions.

This book is intended to engage students in interesting and meaningful language and literature work within realistic contexts appropriate to 13 - 14 year old concerns.

There are 12 units, each one about a different subject. Every unit starts with a lead-in for all students and then encourages different activities for students working at widely different attainment levels. The text is presented as a double-page spread for ease of use, and is suitable for all abilities.

① Core activities are highlighted by the use of coloured circles, and there are extension activities for further work.

Extra support material for all the units can be found in the accompanying Teachers' book, all of which is photocopiable.

☆ A star symbol in the text indicates that relevant material is available to support weaker students, extend the advanced ones, as extra resources or to provide further structure to the work in the text. There are extra sheets, not attached to units.

English is presented as a unified subject in which language work arises naturally and meaningfully in context. We have included complete texts rather than extracts where possible, and drawn on accessible works from major writers of the past.

Terry Brown
Mike Fleming

Folens books are protected by international copyright laws. All rights reserved. The copyright of all materials in this book, except where otherwise stated, remains the property of the publisher and author(s). No part of this publication may be reproduced, stored in a retrieval system, or transmitted, in any form or by any means, for whatever purpose, without the written permission of Folens Limited.

© 1991 Folens Limited, on behalf of the authors.

First published 1991 by Folens Limited, Dunstable and Dublin.

Folens Limited, Albert House, Apex Business Centre, Boscombe Road, Dunstable LU5 4RL, England.

ISBN 1 85276091-5

Contents

Theme 1 Dreams
1.1 Dreams 4
1.2 REM 6
1.3 Day-dreams 8
1.4 Nightmares 10

Theme 2 Encounters
2.1 Encounters 12
2.2 Enough Is Too Much Already 14

Theme 3 Survival
3.1 Survival 20
3.2 To Build a Fire 22
3.3 Living 120 Years 24
3.4 Survival in Communities 26

Theme 4 What's so Funny?
4.1 What's so Funny? 28
4.2 Satire 30
4.3 Parody 32
4.4 Why Do We Laugh? 34

Theme 5 In the News
5.1 In the News 36
5.2 Different Versions 38
5.3 Presenting News 40
5.4 Fair and Honest? 42

Theme 6 What's Your Opinion?
6.1 What's Your Opinion? 44
6.2 The Flute Player 46
6.3 A Formal Debate 50

Theme 7 Perceptions
7.1 Perceptions 52
7.2 Seeing Yourself 54
7.3 The Perception Transfer 56
7.4 Metaphor 58

Theme 8 It's Your Life
8.1 It's Your Life! 60
8.2 Remembering People 62
8.3 Structure and Style 64
8.4 Other People's Lives 66

Theme 9 Writing For Children
9.1 Writing for Children 68
9.2 The Story Teller 70
9.3 Writing a Story 74

Theme 10 On the Road
10.1 On the Road 76
10.2 Homeless 78

Theme 11 Manipulating Language
11.1 Manipulating Language 82
11.2 Say What You Mean! 84
11.3 Word Associations 86

Theme 12 Own Reading
12.1 Own Reading 88
12.2 The Mysteries of . . . 90
12.3 Starting Points 94

1.1 Dreams.

In this unit you will be thinking about dreams and their significance. You will also gain practice in imaginative and informative writing and the use of paragraphs.

Dreams have a considerable fascination for us all and people usually talk about the subject endlessly. Before you start, jot down your own thoughts on the following questions and write more questions of your own. Keep these notes so that you can look at them after any work you do in this unit to see whether your ideas have changed.

- Does everyone dream?
- Have you ever had a dream of falling?
- Are dreams important?
- Can dreams foretell the future?
- Have you ever walked in your sleep?

- Does food you eat cause you to dream?
- Can people dream in colour?
- What causes dreams?
- Do animals dream?
- Is it easy to remember your dreams?

A

① Describe a dream which you can remember well or imagine that the scene shown in **A** is from someone's dream. Write a short account in the past tense and start your account as follows, "Last night I had a strange dream..."

② Rewrite the dream in the present tense capturing more the actual quality of the dream and the way you felt. Include extra details to make the account more vivid.
E.g. *The water is freezing cold as it swirls about my head. Through the dark water two bulging eyes appear like bright headlamps. But they are not in the water ...*

Theme 1: Dreams

Much has been written about dreams but there is no real agreement about their importance or how they are caused. **B** is a list of some of the main ideas.

B
- ✓ Dreams are caused by what we eat.
- ✓ Dreams are memories of what happened in the past.
- ✓ Dreams foretell the future.
- ✓ Dreams are wish fulfilment. (The way we would like things to be).
- ✓ Dreams express our fears and anxieties.

3 ☆ In pairs go through the explanations in **B** and say whether each one sounds convincing or not. Have you, or has anyone you know, had a dream which would fit in with the explanations given here?

The idea that dreams express fears and anxieties is likely to be true for at least some people and some dreams. **C** is one example of such a dream:

C

Actual situation: A man has had a particularly trying day: his car would not start in the morning; when he got to work he found that he had forgotten the key to his office and had to get the caretaker to let him in. He also had an argument with his boss over an important letter to a client which he forgot to put in the post.

His dream: He is driving along a country road when the car gradually comes to a halt of its own accord. The steering wheel comes off in his hands and turns into a snake. His chair starts to recline. He throws the wheel to one side and tries to get out but the door is locked and will not budge. A face, ugly and distorted, presses against the window...

Now try . . . . . .

4 Continue the dream in **C**. The relationship between the reality and the dream does not have to be that obvious. Make the dream a strange combination of possible and impossible events.

5 Attempt to explain the relationship between the dream and the real situation. There may be parts of the dream that cannot be explained.

6 ☆ Imagine that someone has committed a crime and they have such strong feelings of guilt that they walk and talk in their sleep. They are seen and overheard by two other people living in the house. In groups of three write the sleep walking scene in play form.

1.2 REM.

A

People have long wondered what dreams mean. Sigmund Freud was the first scientist to study dreams seriously. His dreams research laid the foundation for the study called psychoanalysis. His book written at the end of the 19th century called "The Interpretation of Dreams" is still considered a scientific masterpiece.

In 1952, a scientist called Eugene Aserinsky, studying the way babies sleep, noticed that at certain times babies' eyes move rapidly beneath the closed lids. He called these times REM (rapid eye movement) periods. We now know that everyone has REM periods during sleep and that it is in these times that we dream. By studying REM periods, we have found out a great deal about sleep. If people are wakened at the start of each REM period, they soon become tired, irritable and nervous when they are awake. As soon as they are allowed to sleep without interruption they become normal again. So it seems we need dreams to stay mentally healthy.

Scientists have found that sleep has quite a complicated pattern. An average man sleeps for about eight hours a night. One to two hours of this time is spent dreaming. First there is a light sleep, then deeper sleep. His muscles relax, his breathing rate and heartbeat decrease, and his body temperature falls slightly. Also the electrical activity of the brain decreases. This can be recorded with an instrument called an electroencephalograph or EEG. This shows that he is not thinking actively.

At the end of the deep sleep period comes a REM period, with dreams and intense mental activity. Then a deep, dreamless period follows and then a dreaming period and so on through the night.

1 You have been asked to edit and improve the style and presentation of the passage **A** for inclusion in a book about dreams.
Some suggestions to help you:
- Give it an eye-catching title.
- Give each paragraph a subtitle.
- Draw diagrams to go with paragraphs three and four.
- Decide which parts, if any, should be left out.
- Are there any alterations to the style of the passage you would make?
- Would a question and answer format have more impact?

2 Think of different ways scientists might start finding out about dreams. Consider different experiments which might be conducted to find out :
- whether physical things which happen to people in their sleep influence their dreams (e.g. alarm goes off)
- whether the things people say in their sleep have any significance
- how often people dream during a night's sleep.

3 Keep a dream diary. A pencil and paper by your bed is useful to write down your dream as soon as you wake up. It is important to do it straight away as most dreams are lost from memory very quickly.

Theme 1: Dreams

EXAMPLES OF DREAMS

Books and magazines which claim to give the exact meaning of dreams are misleading. Not only is there no real agreement about the importance of dreams but the significance of any particular dream will depend on the associations the events have for the person who has had the dream. However, it is possible to list common types of dreams and what they might possibly be symbolising.

Climbing a Mountain	Climbing could symbolise trying to achieve some sort of ambition. If the top is never reached this could mean a feeling of unfulfilment on the part of the dreamer.
Flying	This dream may be associated with a desire to rise above problems which are being experienced or simply a desire to be noticed. Flying suggests rising above one's normal circumstances.
Falling	This is quite a common dream. It is interesting that we use the term "falling" in a figurative way e.g. "falling asleep" or "falling in love". Dreams of falling could have a physical reason; our blood pressure falls as we drop off to sleep. Otherwise the dream could refer to a fear of failure or may be associated with sexual feelings.
Teeth Falling Out	This dream may be experienced as an adult as a memory of when the first teeth fell out. It could therefore be associated with a feeling of growing up, of passing from childhood to adulthood.
Exhibitionist Dreams	The dream of being naked or not properly dressed in public may reflect a wish to overcome feelings of shyness, a desire to be more open with people.

4 After reading the information on this page, make some suggestions for what the following dreams might be symbolising:
being chased, missing a train, looking for a room, floating on air.

5 Invent a dream for each of the people in the following situations. Describe the dream simply in four or five sentences.
- ✓ A young person is moving house with her family but is worried about losing her friends and starting a new school.
- ✓ A business man is in line for promotion but there are two people likely to be promoted before him.
- ✓ A pupil is about to take examinations in school and is tempted to cheat.

6 Choose one of the situations and dreams on this page to use as the basis for a more detailed description. Try to capture the bizarre and illogical nature of dreams in what you write.

Now try . . . . . .

7 In groups plan, write and edit a pamphlet on **Dreams**. Use any information in this unit but try to do some research of your own as well.

1.3 Day-dreams.

Sometimes our minds can wander during the day and we can become lost in pleasant thoughts or fantasies. In the following poem the office worker is struck by the sight of an ice cart and it distracts him from the heat of the city as he day-dreams.

The Ice Cart

Perched on my city office-stool
I watched with envy while a cool
And lucky carter handled ice...
And I was wandering in a trice
Far from the grey and grimy heat
Of that intolerable street
O'er sapphire berg and emerald floe,
Beneath the still cold ruby glow
Of everlasting Polar night,
Bewildered by the queer half-light,
Until I stumbled unawares
Upon a creek where big white bears
Plunged headlong down with flourished heels,
And floundered after shining seals
Through shivering seas of blinding blue.
And, as I watched them, ere I knew
I'd stripped and I was swimming too
Among the seal-pack, young and hale,
And thrusting on with threshing tail,
With twist and twirl and sudden leap
Through crackling ice and salty deep,
Diving and doubling with my kind
Until, at last, we left behind
Those big white blundering bulks of death,
And lay at length with panting breath
Upon a far untravelled floe
Beneath a gentle drift of snow
Snow drifting gently fine and white
Out of the endless Polar night,
Falling and falling evermore
Upon that far untravelled shore
Till I was buried fathoms deep
Beneath that cold white drifting sleep
Sleep drifting sleep,
Deep drifting sleep...

The carter cracked a sudden whip:
I clutched my stool with startled grip,
Awakening to the grimy heat
Of that intolerable street.

W.W. Gibson

Theme 1: Dreams

① Imagine that you have been asked to make a short film for television to accompany a reading of this poem.
- You have noticed that the stages of the man's dream are marked by different verbs: *wandering, stumbled, stripped, lay, buried.*
- Represent the day-dream in five boxes with drawings or brief explanations of what happens at each stage of the day-dream, including a suggestion for each film sequence.

② The dream of the office worker contrasts with the heat of the city. How are you going to emphasise that contrast in your film sequence?
- Make a list of the details in the poem which convey a feeling of coolness.
- Look particularly at the references to colour in the poem and try to develop your ideas for film sequence using colour to emphasise the feeling you desire.

☆ REMINDER - Choice of Verbs

Verbs are key words in any writing. It is easy to use the first verb that comes into your head and then to add an adverb or two to show what you really mean; but that is the lazy way. If you choose the right verb you will not need to add any modifying words; your meaning will be clear immediately.

W. W. Gibson is very careful to choose verbs which convey particular impressions. Consider the verb *stumbled* which gives the impression of clumsy, sudden movement; or the verb *plunged* which suggests the deep dive of the polar bears; or *floundered* which tells us more than just its dictionary definition "to move with difficulty".

Read the poem again and find some others.

In order to find the exact word you need, try using a Thesaurus. This is a form of dictionary which lists words with similar, but not exactly the same, meanings.

Now try . . . . . .

③ Plan a piece of writing of your own in which a person finds some escape by dreaming of another place. The dream could be brought on by the sight of some simple object. Examples:
✓ A pupil in school in a stuffy examination room looks out of the window, sees a kite in the distance and dreams of flying.
✓ A prisoner in a small cell sees a seagull outside and dreams of wide open spaces on a beach.

Follow closely the format in *The Ice Cart* and plan using the following stages:
- Decide exactly where the person is and what they are doing.
- What causes the day-dream? What happens in the dream?
- What makes them return to the real world?

After you have made your plan decide whether you wish to write in poetry or prose.

1.4 Nightmares.

When dreams become particularly distressing or frightening they turn into nightmares.

The Nightmare

Once, as in the darkness I lay asleep by night
Strange things suddenly saw I in my dream;
All my dream was of monsters that came about me while I slept,
Devils and demons, four-horned, serpent-necked,
Fishes with bird-tails, three-legged bogies   5
From six eyes staring; dragons hideous,
Yet three-part human.
On rushed the foul flocks, grisly legions,
Stood round me, stretched out their arms,
Danced their hands about me, and sought to snatch me from my bed.   10
Then I cried (and in my dream
My voice was thick with anger and my words all awry),
"Ill-spawned elves, how dare you
Beset with your dire shapes Creation's cleanest
Shapeliest creature, Man?" Then straightaway I struck out,   15
Flashed my fists like lightning among them, thumped like thunder,
Here slit Jack-o'-Lantern,
Here smashed fierce Hog-Face,
Battered wights and goblins,
Smote venturous vampires, pounded in the dust   20
Imps, gnomes and lobs,
Kobolds and kelpies;
Swiped bulge-eyed bogies, oafs and elves;
Clove Tough-head's triple skull, threw down
Clutching Night-hag, flogged the gawky Ear-wig Fiend   25
That floundered toward me on its tail.

I struck at staring eyes,
Stamped on upturned faces; through close ranks
Of hoofs I cut my way, buried my fingers deep
In half-formed flesh;   30
Ghouls tore at my touch; I slit sharp noses,
Trod on red tongues, seized shaggy manes,
Shook bald-heads by the beard.
Then was scuffling. Arms and legs together
Chasing, crashing and sliding, a helter-skelter   35
Of feet lost and found in the tugging and toppling,
Cuffing, cudgelling, frenzied, flogging...

So fought I, till terror and dismay
Shook those foul flocks; panic spread like a flame
Down mutinous ranks; they stand, they falter,   40
Those ghastly legions; but fleeing, suddenly turn
Glazed eyes upon me, to see how now I fare.

Theme 1: Dreams

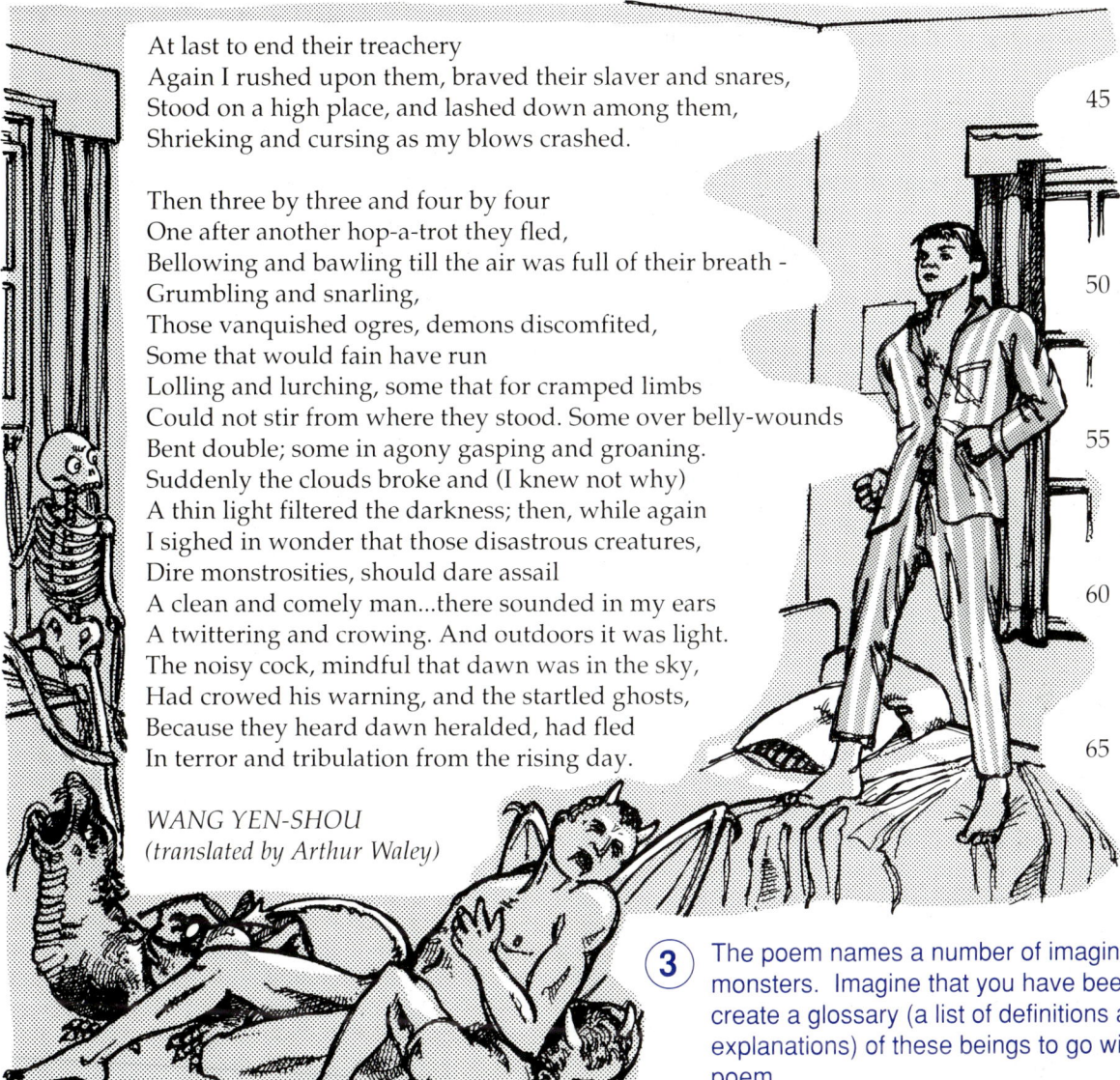

At last to end their treachery
Again I rushed upon them, braved their slaver and snares,
Stood on a high place, and lashed down among them,   45
Shrieking and cursing as my blows crashed.

Then three by three and four by four
One after another hop-a-trot they fled,
Bellowing and bawling till the air was full of their breath -
Grumbling and snarling,   50
Those vanquished ogres, demons discomfited,
Some that would fain have run
Lolling and lurching, some that for cramped limbs
Could not stir from where they stood. Some over belly-wounds   55
Bent double; some in agony gasping and groaning.
Suddenly the clouds broke and (I knew not why)
A thin light filtered the darkness; then, while again
I sighed in wonder that those disastrous creatures,
Dire monstrosities, should dare assail
A clean and comely man...there sounded in my ears   60
A twittering and crowing. And outdoors it was light.
The noisy cock, mindful that dawn was in the sky,
Had crowed his warning, and the startled ghosts,
Because they heard dawn heralded, had fled   65
In terror and tribulation from the rising day.

WANG YEN-SHOU
(translated by Arthur Waley)

1 This is an ideal poem for reading aloud but it needs careful preparation.
- In groups of 3 or 4 decide how you are going to read it - who will read which lines?
- It is also important to decide which lines will be spoken loudly, which softly and where the reading should slowly get louder or softer.
- It can be very effective to use music playing in the background, gradually increasing and decreasing the volume between verses.

2 This poet also selects verbs for very careful effects. List the verbs from line 15 to line 30 and notice how many and varied they are.

3 The poem names a number of imaginary monsters. Imagine that you have been asked to create a glossary (a list of definitions and explanations) of these beings to go with the poem.
- Choose five of the creatures mentioned in the poem and write a description to go with each one.
- Start with any information you are given in the poem but use your imagination to extend the description:
  ✓ What do they look like?
  ✓ What powers do they have?
  ✓ Where are they supposed to live?

Now try . . . . . .

4 Write your own piece about a nightmare which has as one of its main stylistic features the effective use of verbs. This could be a poem if you wish.

2.1 Encounters.

In this unit you will be looking at human interaction - the way people relate to each other.

HOW WELL DO YOU KNOW YOUR FRIEND?

① Work in pairs or in groups of 3 to answer the following questions about your partner. When you have all finished, exchange your sets of answers and correct your partner's ideas where necessary. We refer to the person being questioned as X.
- What are X's hobbies?
- What makes X angry?
- What is X's favourite food?
- What is X's favourite T.V. programme?
- If X had a free choice regardless of cost, where would s/he choose to go on a 2-week holiday?
- What does X want to do when s/he leaves school?
- Does X support a football team? If so, which?
- What frightens X?
- What is X's favourite pop singer or group?
- If X were to appear on *Mastermind*, what would s/he choose for her/his specialist subject?

Theme 2: Encounters

When you have corrected your partner's ideas about you, award her or him a grade as follows:

S/he knows you

A - very well   **C** - not very well
B - well   **D** - hardly at all!

Although the answers to these questions do tell us something about a person, you may think that some of them give information which is not very important. Which do you think are the most revealing questions, and why?

If you really know a person, you should be able to answer much more profound questions. For example: if your friend was able to get a new law passed in the United Kingdom, what would it be? Questions like that, answered honestly, will tell us a lot about a person.

2 Work out 6 questions which, if answered honestly, would tell us a lot about a person and compare lists.
- In groups of 4, work out an agreed list of 10 questions which together could reveal much about a person.
- Display the agreed lists for general discussion.
- Now, choose ONE of these lists and answer all the questions about yourself.
- You may wish to keep your answers secret, or you may decide to let a limited audience see them.

INVENTING CHARACTERS

When Arthur Ransome was a young and struggling author, he was given a piece of advice which he found very useful.

An older writer told him that when he was creating a fictional character for one of his books he should always invent some things about the character which he was NOT going to use in the story.

If he did that, Ransome was told, then his readers would believe in the characters because they would seem like real people.

Try it! Make up lots of things about your characters even if you cannot use all of the details.

Now try . . . . . .

3 Invent 2 characters who do not know each other at this stage; they are going to meet each other later on. It is entirely up to you what sort of people they are, but you will need to make notes about all the following in each case.
- Name
- Age
- Physical appearance
- Home background
- Work background
- Hobbies
- Personality - friendly, bad-tempered, introverted, etc.
- Friends
- Any details which have influenced the person strongly

2.2 Enough Is...

When 2 people meet for the first time, circumstances and the sort of people they are can cause strange things to happen. The following story, *Enough Is Too Much Already*, by Jan Mark will be read most effectively by 4 people taking the parts of the narrator, Maurice, Nina and Nazzer.

"Look", Maurice said, "lay off, will you? I've told you I'm sorry, haven't I? I mean, I mean it. I am sorry."

"You look it," Nazzer said. "You look so sorry my heart bleeds for you. Doesn't he look sorry?" said Nazzer, turning to Nina for confirmation. "Tears pouring down his little face."

"We waited outside for half an hour," Nina said. "It was freezing. Real brass monkeys. Cardy says she's not interested any more. We only asked her because you said you fancied her. Now she thinks I've been sending her up. Cardy's my best friend," Nina said. "Was."

"If you'd been in my position," Maurice began.

"Catch me in any position you'd be in," said Nina. "Next time you get your eye on a girl, you do your own fishing."

"I'm not making excuses," said Maurice. "I've got a reason. I was unavoidably delayed. Nah, shut up, Nina, I'm trying to tell you. You know I nearly missed the train last night -"

"How should I know?"

"Because it was you kept me hanging about trying to set me up for Cardy -"

"I like that! You were the one -"

"I only suggested that she might like -"

"The way you go on anyone would think they were forming queues -"

"If you'll only listen," Maurice said.

"I mean, you think you look so glorious -"

"Lady, give the guy a chance," Nazzer pleaded. "Turn down the goddam volume, willya?"

"Well I did."

"What?"

"Nearly miss the train. It was about twenty-five past when I got to the station, and I'm just running on to the platform when old Patterson looms up like King Kong, out of a rubbish bin. I reckon he was trying to fish out the Sun while no-one was looking. 'Ho, Nicholls,' he says, 'didn't we have a little appointment at lunchtime?' and we had had, only I'd forgotten, and I said, 'I can't stop now, Sir. I'll miss me train,' and he started saying something, and the geezer on the public address started bawling something about a platform change, and would we all please pay attention, so I couldn't hear a word anyway -"

"Nobody can hear a word old Patterson says," Nazzer remarked.

"- and old Patterson's still going on, so I just said, 'Yes Sir, sorry Sir,' and ran like hell and jumped on the train."

"I heard," Nina said. "You don't have to tell me. It was on the news, this morning. Maurice Nicholls caught his train. Norwich rocked to its foundations. Right before the earthquake in China, it was. And the Third World War breaking out."

"Well, it looked all right, and I sat down, and got my physics out, like I was meant to have given Patterson at dinner-time, when this girl gets on."

"I hope you don't think I'm going to tell Cardy all this?" Nina said. "I mean this is going to make her feel really marvellous, isn't it?"

"No, give it a rest," Maurice said. "I didn't really see her at first. I just noticed these legs going by."

"Oh. Legs," Nazzer murmured, into his coffee. "Legs."

"Not what you think, Naz. You got a scaly mind. She was wearing those horrible wrinkly leg-warmers that look like lagging on old water pipes," Maurice said.

"Thanks a million," Nina said, peering under the table and adjusting something through her skirt.

"And anyway, she goes and stands up the front with all the other Red Berets -"

"Oh, a St. Ursula's Virgin," said Nazzer. "Legs ..."

"They all wear those short leg-warmers that only come up to your knees," Nina said. "It's some soft sort of fashion, or something. They always fall down."

"- and she starts chatting to them, and then I see Langham up front, too."

"Langham doesn't go on your train."

"That's what I thought, and I'm just about to go up and say, 'Get your great greasy body off our train, Langham,' when he gets up for something, and she steps back and treads on his foot."

"Yes?"

"What?"

"What happened?"

"Nothing happened," Nazzer droned. "You could drop a breeze-block on Langham's foot and he wouldn't notice.

You could drop a breeze-block on his head -"

"He noticed, all right. He lets out this great horrible roar - you know, that sort of Wrrroagh! noise you get at First Division matches, and she turns round and

Theme 2: Encounters

says, 'Oh, I'm sorry. Did I hurt you?' She had a nice voice," Maurice reported, mournfully.

"And Langham starts mincing about and flapping his hands and squeaking, 'Ooooh, Ai'm sorreigh. Did Ai hurt yaw?' and then the train starts - you know how those little pay trains jolt when they start."

"They're only buses on rails," Nazzer said. "If they did away with the bridges they could have double-decker pay trains."

"- and she falls against him, and he yells, 'Oh, oh, she's after me, look, she fancies me, ooh-ooh-ooh!' and starts pulling her about, and she gives him a shove, and I can see him getting nasty -"

"Getting?" Nina said. "He's a fat horrible pig, that Langham."

"Well, I thought, someone'll stop it, but all the old geezers thought it was just kids mucking about, and let him get on with it. You know, she was really upset; you could see that, but they just went on reading the paper and looking out of the windows. I could just imagine them all sitting and watching a murder, like it was something on telly, and not doing anything about it."

"What 'bout the other Virgins?"

"Oh, I thought they'd do something, you know, I mean ... there were six of them, but they just giggled a bit and looked the other way, and one of them said, 'Some people'll do anything to get a bit of attention,' and someone else says,'Oh, her,' real snarky. And she tried to pull away from him, but he got her by the strap of her bag -"

"This is getting really exciting," said Nina. "Isn't it, Naz? Don't you wish you could stay for the end?"

"It wasn't funny. You wouldn't have thought it was funny if it had been you. She had the strap wrapped round her wrist, and he kept twisting it - you know what a great lunk he is, Naz -"

"Why do people keep asking me?" said Nazzer.

"You pulled out of the Second Eleven because of Langham," Maurice said. "And this Cilla was only a small little thing."

"Oh, Cilla, was it?"

"You know her?"

"No, but I mean - Cilla."

"'Sno dafter than Nina," Nazzer said morosely, inspecting the bottom of his cup.

"I don't know how you've lived so long, Nazzer."

"She was starting to cry, and the train was shaking around all over the points, and she nearly fell on me."

"She seems to fall on a lot of people, this Cilla," Nina remarked.

"So I got up and tapped Langham on the back of the neck -"

"Langham hasn't got a neck," Nazzer said. "His head grows out of his deltoids."

"Watch your language," Nina said.

"- with the edge of my physics book, and I said, 'Lay off, Langham,' and he looks at me and says, 'You're going the long way home, aren't you?' I thought he was being cryptic, meaning, I'm going to duff you up, shortly, but I said, 'Lay off, Langham, will you, or I shall have to rearrange you,' and he said, 'You and whose army?' "

"He would," Nazzer said. "I've never heard him come out with anything original; I don't reckon he was being cryptic, you know. He's not really programmed for it."

"So, I got my physics book and hit him behind the left knee."

"Why the left knee?"

"He couldn't reach any higher," Nazzer explained.

"The left knee is a vulnerable spot on Langham, right now," Maurice said, "since Saturday's match. You know what it's like, first match of the Autumn Term. There was a lot of old scores settled on Saturday; sort of backlog left over from Easter. Someone reckoned up with Langham's left leg. Anyway, it worked. He went over backwards, sort of Z-shaped. I wish you could have seen him, Naz. It would have made up for a lot."

"I'll think about it in Maths," Nazzer said. "It'll cheer me up no end."

"So, I said to this girl, this Cilla, 'Come on, let's get down the other end,' and she said, 'Supposing he follows us?' so I said, 'I can always pull the emergency chain.' "

"That's what Superman does, you know," said Nazzer.

"When Lois Lane's in peril, he flies to the rescue and pulls the emergency chain. And the emergency bog flushes," he added.

"I was joking," Maurice said, heavily. "So anyway, we sort of stepped over Langham, and all these old geezers and ladies were sucking their false choppers, and old Langham was groaning, and this Cilla, she looks at me like I was Superman. I mean, it wasn't bad going, was it? I mean, it was Langham, and I did thump him."

"What did the virgins do?"

"Nothing. But they looked a bit envious," Maurice conceded, modestly.

"He's not at school today," Nina said.

"Maybe you killed him," said Nazzer.

"Well he didn't come after us, did he?" Maurice said. "He couldn't. No, I didn't kill him. I saw him get off at Brundall. He was limping."

"Brundall?"

"He lives at Brundall."

15

Enough Is Too Much Already.

"But you were on the Sheringham train."

"Well, that's it, you see," Maurice said. "We weren't. We just arrived at the back end of the train, when we got to the place where the Sheringham line breaks off, and I noticed we weren't on it. I mean, the track had branched off, but the train was still on the Yarmouth line."

"So that's where you were," Nina said. "Yarmouth! I'm not telling Cardy. You'd better think of something better, or something."

"No! It wasn't like that. See, I realised then that I'd got on the wrong train, so I thought, well, I'll get off at Brundall, then I thought, no I won't, that's where Langham gets off - I'll get off at Buckenham. And so we get to Brundall and I see old Langham falling about on the platform - you would have enjoyed it, Naz - and then the conductor comes along, and I realised I'd only got my season to Worstead, and it's not even on that line, and this girl, Cilla, she's still sitting next to me, sniffing, and I don't know where she's getting off, and I don't want to lose sight of her yet. So anyway, the conductor gets to us, and I say, politely, 'You first,' and she hums and hahs a bit, and the conductor says, 'Where to darling?' and in the end she says, 'Reedham,' and she blushes a bit, and says, 'I don't really live there. I'm just going to see someone.'"

He gives her a ticket.

"I say, 'Can I come with you?' and she giggles and says, 'Better not; it's my auntie.'

" 'And what about you?' says the conductor, to me.

"Well I was stuck wasn't I? I mean, we were just coming in to Buckenham, but I couldn't get off before she did. I didn't know her name or where she lived, or anything."

"I thought you said her name was Cilla," Nina snapped.

"Yes, but I didn't know that yet, did I? I had to find out, didn't I? And I ask you; Reedham! It's like the end of the world. And I said, 'Berney Arms,' because that's the next station after Reedham, and he says, 'This train don't go to Berney Arms. This is the Lowestoft train.' "

"I thought you said it was going to Yarmouth," Nina said.

"It's the same line till Reedham," Maurice said.

"So I looked a right nutter, didn't I, and I said, 'Oh, then I'll go on to Haddiscoe and borrow me brother-in-law's bike,' so he gives me a ticket."

"Your brother-in-law's out on the rigs, isn't he?" Nazzer said.

"His bike isn't."

"No, his bike's in the garage down Earlham Road," said Nina.

"The conductor didn't know that, did he?" Maurice said. "Look, I was lying, for God's sake. I just wanted to find out a bit more about her. That's natural isn't it?"

"If you say so."

"I s'pose you'd forgot about us," Nina said.

"Well...it was only ten to five, then. I hadn't even started thinking about you. So we got talking, and she says she's only just started at St. Ursula's, and her name's Cilla Hales, and she lives in Wymondham, and I think that's brilliant, because the Wymondham train goes at five-twenty, so I can see her every evening, and then get the six o'clock home. Then we stop at Cantley, and all the other Virgins get out - what d'you think so many of them could be doing in Cantley? They can't all be Catholics out there -"

"There's nothing else to do," Nazzer said, "except the beet refinery, but that doesn't open till Monday."

"Anyway, they all get out, and Cilla ducks her head down and says, 'Stupid stuck-up cows,' and then we talked a bit, and we're nearly at Reedham, and she's getting ready to go. So I say, 'I'll see you tomorrow, shall I?' and she says, 'Oh yes. Thanks ever so for - you know what,' and I say, 'Well, it was nothing. Let's meet in the buffet for coffee,' and she says, 'O.K, let's,' and then we're in Reedham.

"So. She got off, and waved at me from the platform as the train moved off. I hoped her auntie was meeting her, because the mist was coming down really thick. Oh God, it's like the end of the world, Reedham, it's like the end of the Universe."

"End of the universe is a time, not a place," Nazzer said.

"Time and place are the same thing," Nina said. "Old Patterson told us."

"That's Time and Space."

"It's right on the edge of the marshes -"

"What is?"

"Reedham."

"I know," Nazzer said. "My mum took me there for a picnic when I was a young lad. I fell in a dyke and nearly drowned."

"Are you sure they got you out in time?" Nina said. "Brain death can occur after four minutes. I mean you might have got left under for five."

"Brain damage, not brain death," Nazzer said. "Brain death's when they pull the plug out of your life support system and break you up for spares."

"- at least," Maurice went on, "I thought it was like the end of the world until we got to Haddiscoe. There's nothing at Haddiscoe, just two platforms. There's not even a bridge or a subway - you have to walk across the lines."

16

Theme 2: Encounters

"It's Doomsville, man," said Nazzer.

"Well, I got out of the train, I was the only one, and I stood and watched it going away into the mist - it was getting really thick by now, and I couldn't see anything, just the rear light on the train and the telephone box down the road. Well, I looked at the timetable and there's a train back from Lowestoft at thirty-three minutes past, so I ring me mum and say I won't be home for tea, and I go for a walk. In the mist. All on me tod."

"Thinking about Cilla?" Nazzer played soulful music on an imaginary violin.

"Why not?" Maurice demanded. "I'd done all right, hadn't I? And I was going to see her the next day, so I thought it was worth getting stuck at Haddiscoe. I could hear this horrible noise, a sort of quiet tearing sound. It really frightened me, you know, it was all around. You couldn't see where it was coming from."

"Don't think I've ever seen a noise," Nina said.

"You ever been out in the garden at night and listened to the snails eating the lettuces? It was like that, only about a hundred times louder. Well, I walked around a bit, and went back to the station and waited, and the train didn't come and didn't come, and I thought they must have cancelled it. It was bloody cold, I can tell you, Naz - you'd never think it was only September."

"We were cold too, weren't we, Naz?" Nina said.

"Anyway, it came in the end - I could hear it for ages before I could see it, and I got on."

"What was the tearing noise?" Nazzer asked.

"Cows eating the grass," Maurice said. "They were all over the place. I think they must go on eating all night, all the year round.

"Well, I sat on the train, and it was crawling along, because of the mist, and I was perishing cold, but I didn't really mind - I was thinking about Cilla. And then the train stopped at Reedham, and the door opened, and there she was."

"Who?"

"Lois Lane," said Nazzer.

"Cilla. Her. She came and sat down right opposite me and I thought, ere ere, and then she looked up and saw me. She went right pink - then green," Maurice said.

"So I said, 'That was a short visit, wasn't it?' and she said, 'What happened to your brother-in-law's bike?' real snarky.

"And I said, 'Wasn't your auntie in?' and she looked at me all funny and says, 'Was your brother-in-law out?'

"And then she said, 'You got straight back on the train, didn't you? You don't live round here at all, do you? Not even at Berney Arms,' and I said, 'No, well, actually I live at Worstead.'

"She said, 'Why were you going to Haddiscoe?'

"And I said, 'I didn't want to get off the train before you did. I wanted to stay with you a bit longer,' but it didn't work. She said, 'But Worstead's on the other line,' and I said, 'I got on the wrong train.' She said, 'Well, why didn't you get off it?' and I said, 'Like I said, I wanted to stay with you till you got out.' And she said, 'I was on the wrong train too. I only got on to give my mate a book and that fat fella jumped on me.'

"And I said, 'Well, I saved you, didn't I?' and she said, 'You might have said something. We could have got off at Brundall and hitched back.'

"And I said, 'You mean, you only stayed on because of me?'

"And she said 'You mean you stayed on because of me?' and I said 'Yes.'

"And she said, 'Blast you! I've missed the Wymondham train and there isn't another till half-past eight.'

"And I said, 'Well I can't get one till eight, either - that's nearly as bad. Let's have a coffee in the buffet at Norwich,' and she said, 'Bugger the buffet. My mum'll go spare when I get in,' and she got up and went all the way to the other end of the train. I watched her all the way."

Nina said, "Is that all?"

"All?" Maurice echoed. "Isn't that enough?"

"Too much," Nazzer murmured. "Did you see her again?"

"In the distance," Maurice said, "and I saw her in the buffet at Norwich, but she wouldn't talk to me. When I sat down she got up and walked to another table...So I followed her, and she got up and moved again, and I went over and said, 'I don't know why you're so angry,' and she said 'I suppose you think it's funny,' and I said 'Yes,' and she said, 'That's why I'm angry,' and got up and found another table. She kept on doing it. It was like musical chairs. In the end I went out and got my train - and then I found I'd left my school bag with my season and all on Haddiscoe Station. The cows have probably eaten it by now. My physics was in there too.

"Anyway, that's why I didn't come to the disco last night." said Maurice.

Enough Is Too Much Already.

The style of this story is interesting. It is told ENTIRELY in conversation between 3 people. The writer hardly intervenes at all to tell you anything except who is speaking and occasionally how they speak. Yet, despite being told nothing about the 3 characters, at the end of the story we do know a lot about them. For example, Nina and Nazzer react very differently to Maurice's story.

1. Write a paragraph each about what Nina and Nazzer think of Maurice's story, giving your evidence.

2. Choose one of the characters - Maurice, Nina or Nazzer.
   - What sort of person is s/he? Funny, sarcastic, clever, understanding?
   - Would you find it easy to make friends with them?
   - Write down 6-8 statements about your chosen character, giving evidence from the story for your statement in each case.

3. If you had to choose one as a friend, who would it be? Why?

4. Nina and Nazzer keep interrupting the flow of Maurice's story by going off on tangents. Find two examples of this.

☆ REMINDER - Punctuating Direct Speech.

It is useful to remember that you do not always need to put in who is speaking when writing direct speech; that is often obvious from the context.

If you leave out the *he said - she said* words, then punctuation of direct speech is easy. You just follow the usual rules:

✓ only one person should speak in any one paragraph
✓ start each new speech with a capital letter
✓ and make sure that ALL SPEECH is inside the inverted commas.

If you need to write in who is speaking, check that you have punctuated it correctly by looking back at *Enough Is Too Much Already*. There are examples there of all the constructions you are likely to use.

Now try . . . . . .

5. Just suppose, some days later, that Cilla regretted snubbing Maurice and sent a message to him via Nina. Write another episode of the story when Nina meets Maurice and Nazzer and (eventually) gives Maurice the message from Cilla. Use the same style - tell it all in direct speech. Your discussion about the 3 characters should help you; Nina doesn't take such matters as seriously as the other 2.

6. You could try role-playing your scene once you had worked out together what the message was.

7. ☆ How do you ask a person of the opposite sex to go out with you? What advice would you give to someone who asked you this question?

8. Once you have sorted out some advice, write a short scene between two people in which your advice is followed. Did it work?

Theme 2: Encounters

There is one more thing you need to consider before using your 2 invented characters in an encounter of their own.

9 Choose 2 of these pictures and, in pairs, discuss what would be your first ideas about the sort of people they are, and how you would react to each of them. Make notes as you go along.
- Your opinions will be tentative, because a picture does not give you much to go on. However, note down your tentative opinions, and also your reasons for them.
- Do any of your opinions depend on an interpretation of some small detail in the picture?

10 Now, on your own, think about meeting a person for the first time.
☆ You need to make some decisions about the person immediately - after all, there are people whom you might greet with a cheery "Hi, there", and there are people with whom you would be more formal.
- What do you look at in order to form tentative ideas about a person? Is it their hairstyle? Their shoes? Whether they smile at you or not?
- Note down what you would look at in this first meeting in order to form tentative ideas about a person. Share the list with a friend and agree on a combined list.
- Then, in pairs, take each item in turn and write down what would encourage you to like the person and what you would take as a warning sign.
- If you are going to display these lists, then set them out as effectively as you can. In any case, it would be helpful if you could all have a look at those produced by other people.

11 Now is the time to take your 2 invented characters and arrange for them to meet. No one can help you very much at this stage, because the circumstances in which they meet depend, in part, on the characters you have invented.
- Try to choose circumstances in which it is possible they would meet, and which could lead to some conflict or development.
- Tell the story of their encounter, keeping true to the characters you have invented.
- You could carry on and develop a story as a project, letting the characters you have invented influence what happens. You will not be in complete control of your own story any more; but it will be fun.

3.1 Survival.

In this unit you will be thinking about various aspects of survival in different types of situations.

The drawings A, B, C and D show 4 people in dangerous situations.

A

B

C

D

1) Imagine that each person could choose one fairly small object (other than food and water) to help them survive. What do you think it should be?

2) Choose one of the situations and imagine that the person survived after a considerable ordeal. In pairs conduct a radio interview in which the survivor tells his or her story in response to questioning.

3) Write the newspaper article and headline which appeared the day after one of the individuals shown in the drawing was rescued.

4) Create a "survival kit" of no more than 7 small items which might have been a valuable aid in one of these situations.

20

Theme 3: Survival

The following passage has been written to be included in a book on survival. Your task is to edit the passage, to improve its style, accuracy and presentation. The tasks printed below will guide you.

> If you find yourself outside in bad weather conditions it may be uncomfortable but it could be worse because it could be extremely dangerous indeed. Some people actually plan to go out in bad weather, others may get caught unexpectedly.
>
> One main danger which faces people who are out in a bad weather is exposure. If to much body heat is lost the consequences can be fatal. The situation becomes worse if clothing becomes wet and is not thick enough to insulate the body and lets in the cold. It is better to take the write precautions than to be faced with the onslaught of exposure. Care should be taken with clothing. If it does not fit properly, flapping cloth can expell warm air. Air can also be lost through openings at the neck and at the ends of sleeves and at the ends of trouser legs. These should be fastened. However it is important, that you do not allow your clothes to become soaked with sweat as the evaporation of sweat will tke away body heat. The effect of wind blowing through clothing and removing body heat is reduced if you have several layers of clothing - even plastic sheeting or newspapers can help. Remember that combination of cold moisture and wind in severe conditions can be fatal. The extremeties of the body (hands, feet head) body heat is lost from and these should be covered. In bad situations shelter should be sought - even a pile of rocks or the trunk of a fallen tree will help. In the snow, a shelter can be made in the snow itself.
>
> It is much better of course to take precautions before you leave so that you are not in a position of having to respondto the unexpected. It is a good idea to let people know where you are going and what route you are planning to take. It is also a good idea to take the right clothers, food for emergengies, etc.

5 Check the passage carefully for accuracy (particularly spelling) and style.
- Decide how many diagrams/drawings you will use to accompany the passage and describe what you require in precise language so that an artist can understand what you want.
- Do you need headings for any of the paragraphs?
- Decide whether any of the items should be printed in capital letters or highlighted.
- How should the passage be presented on the page?
- Draw a diagram to show the position of text and drawings.
- Write a brief introduction to the passage which explains what it is about and give it a title.

Now try . . . . . .

6 You have been asked to write an entry for the book on survival which gives advice on building fires and shelters. You could do some research or else rely on your own common sense and knowledge.

3.2 To Build a Fire.

In Jack London's story *To Build a Fire* a man is out in the wild in dangerously cold weather. He gets wet and knows that he has to build a fire and dry off quickly or he will freeze and die.

And then it happened. At the place where there were no signs, where the soft, unbroken snow seemed to advertise solidity beneath, the man broke through. It was not deep. He wet himself halfway to the knees before he floundered out of the firm crust.

He was angry, and cursed his luck aloud. He had hoped to get into camp with the boys at six o'clock, and this would delay him an hour, for he would have to build a fire and dry out his footgear. This was imperative at that low temperature - he knew that much; and he turned aside to the bank, which he climbed. On top, tangled in the underbrush about the trunks of several small spruce trees, was a high-water deposit of dry fire-wood - sticks and twigs, principally, but also larger portions of seasoned branches of fine, dry, last-year's grasses. He threw down several large pieces on top of the snow. This served for a foundation and prevented the young flame from drowning itself in the snow it otherwise would melt. The flame he got by touching a match to a small shred of birch-bark that he took from his pocket. This burned even more readily than paper. Placing it on the foundation, he fed the young flames with wisps of dry grass and with the tiniest dry twigs. He worked slowly and carefully, keenly aware of his danger. Gradually, as the flame grew stronger, he increased the size of the twigs with which he fed it. He squatted in the snow, pulling the twigs out from their entanglement in the brush and feeding directly to the flame. He knew there must be no failure. When it is seventy-five below zero, a man must not fail in his first attempt to build a fire - that is, if his feet are wet. If his feet are dry, and he fails, he can run along the trail for half a mile and restore his circulation. But the circulation of wet and freezing feet cannot be restored by running when it is seventy-five below. No matter how fast he runs, the wet feet will freeze the harder. All this the man knew. The old-timer on Sulphur Creek had told him about the previous fall, and now he was appreciating the advice. Already all sensation had gone out of his feet. To build the fire he had been forced to remove his mittens, and the fingers had quickly gone numb. His pace of four miles an hour had kept his heart pumping blood to the surface of his body and to all the extremities. But the instant he stopped, the action of the pump eased down. The cold of space smote the unprotected tip of the planet, and he, being on that unprotected tip, received the full force of the blow. The blood of his body recoiled before it. The blood was alive, like the dog, and like the dog it wanted to hide away and cover itself up from the fearful cold. So long as he walked four miles an hour, he pumped that blood, willy-nilly, to the surface; but now it ebbed away and sank down to the recesses of his body. The extremities were the first to feel its absence. His wet feet froze the faster, and his exposed fingers numbed the faster, though they had not yet begun to freeze. Nose and cheeks were already freezing, while the skin of all his body chilled as it lost its blood.

But he was safe. Toes and nose and cheeks would only be touched by the frost, for the fire was beginning to burn with strength. He was feeding it with twigs the size of his finger. In another minute he would be able to feed it with branches the size of his wrist and then he could remove his wet footgear, and while it dried he could keep his naked feet warm by the fire, rubbing them at first, of course, with snow. The fire was a success. He was safe. He remembered the advice of the old-timer on Sulphur Creek, and smiled. The old-timer had been very serious in laying down the law so that no man must travel alone in the Klondike after fifty below. Well, here he was; he had had an accident; he was alone; and he had saved

Theme 3: Survival

himself. Those old-timers were rather womanish, some of them, he thought. All a man had to do was to keep his head, and he was alright. Any man who was a man could travel alone. But it was surprising, the rapidity with which his cheeks and nose were freezing. And he had not thought his fingers could go lifeless in so short a time. Lifeless they were, for he could hardly make them move together to grip a twig, and they seemed remote from his body and from him. When he touched a twig, he had to look and see whether or not he had a hold of it. The wires were pretty well down between him and his finger-ends.

All of which counted for little. There was the fire, snapping and crackling and promising life with every dancing flame. He started to untie his moccasins. They were coated with ice; the thick German socks were like sheaths of iron halfway to his knees; and the moccasin strings were like rods of steel all twisted and knotted as by some conflagration. For a moment he tugged with his numbed fingers, then, realizing the folly of it, he drew his sheath-knife.

But before he could cut the strings, it happened. It was his own fault or, rather, his mistake. He should not have built the fire under the spruce tree. He should have built it out in the open. But it had been easier to pull the twigs from the brush and drop them directly on the fire. Now the tree under which he had done this carried a weight of snow on its boughs. No wind had blown for weeks, and each bough was fully freighted. Each time he pulled a twig he had communicated a slight agitation to the tree - an imperceptible agitation, so far as he was concerned, but an agitation sufficient to bring about the disaster. High up in the tree one bough capsized its load of snow. This fell on the boughs beneath, capsizing them. This process continued, spreading out and involving the whole tree. It grew like an avalanche, and it descended without warning upon the man and the fire, and the fire was blotted out! Where it had burned was a mantle of fresh and disordered snow. The man was shocked. It was as though he had just heard his own sentence of death.

1 Describe the different stages the man goes through in his efforts to build the fire.

2 The success of this piece of writing is partly in the detail which the author includes. Try a similar piece of writing which is equally detailed. You will need to decide on:
- a dangerous situation, e.g. being shipwrecked, trapped in a burning house, hanging from a rope on a mountain, getting stuck on a level crossing in a car with an invalid passenger;
- what the individual needs to do or build in order to survive, e.g. grab hold of a rope which is out of reach, make some sort of rope ladder;
- what goes wrong just at the last minute.

Build the story slowly as in *To Build a Fire* including as much detail as possible.

Now try . . . . . .

3 ☆ Use information contained in the passage and any other knowledge you have to construct a warning notice to people who may be going out in very low temperatures. The notice must be clear and easy to read.

3.3 Living 120 Years.

WHAT IS IT LIKE TO LIVE FOR 120 YEARS?

There are a few small areas in the world where people often live to a great age. Three of these areas are: the village of Vilcabamba and the surrounding area of southern Ecuador; the Abkhasian region in Georgia, USSR; and the Hunza community on the borders of China and Pakistan.

Between 1971 and 1973, David Davies made a study of the people in Vilcabamba and its neighbouring villages. He has written his findings up in a book called *"The Centenarians of the Andes"*. During his travels he met many people who were well over 100 years old. There was Victor Maza, aged 120, whom he photographed hoeing maize on his small-holding. Then there was Gabriel Brazo, also 120, and his wife, a mere stripling of 70 years.

He stopped what he was doing - repairing his shoes - to entertain his guests. Senor Carrion and his wife at a nearby village called La Thoma were respectively 145 and 140 years old; David Davies was informed by the village chief that nowadays they did only the lightest of work around their home.

There seems to have been no doubt about the ages of most of the centenarians whom David Davies met. In many cases he was able to see and photograph their birth certificates. He was also shown the death certificates of 4 people who had died in the 1920s and 1930s, aged 150. He noted two other extraordinary facts.

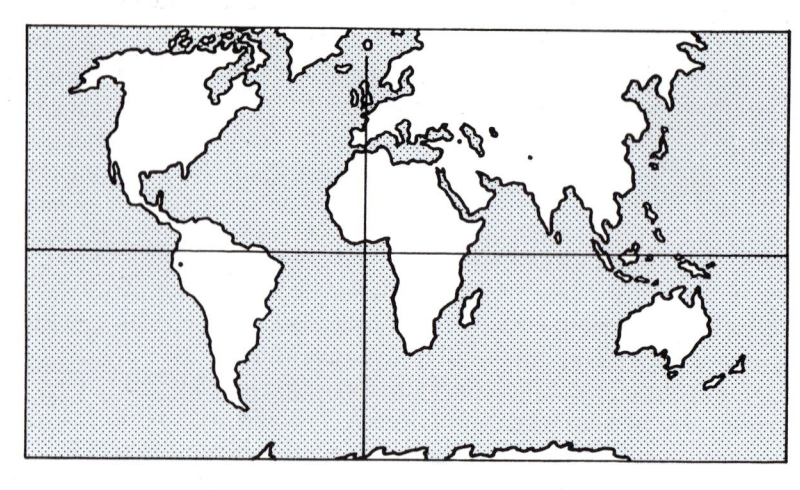

Very old people were not isolated cases, but quite common. In the single village of San Pedro in 1972, 88 people out of the total population of 760 were over 80 years old.

The old people seemed to remain healthy, active, and mentally alert right up to their deaths. The communities were free from the diseases which are common in our country - and in the towns not many miles away from Vilcabamba.

David Davies was a scientist. His main interest in the centenarians was to discover why such large numbers of people in a small geographical area lived to such a great age. He was also concerned to find out how they remained so healthy, active, and mentally alert, in contrast with some sad examples of old people in our own country.

In order to compare the lifestyles, he also studied the people in the other two areas mentioned.

A well-known Abkhasian was Shirali Luslimov who lived in the village of Barzavu. He died in 1973 at the age of 168. His family was an extraordinary one: two of his brothers lived to be 134 and 106; his mother died aged 110 and his father aged 120.

So what did these two groups have in common which might help to explain the phenomenon? He could reach no firm conclusions, but the following do seem to play some part. Diet, especially low calorie intake and absence of obesity; high altitude (the Ecuadorean villages are between 1350 and 1550 metres above sea level); low rainfall; genetic factors - does longevity run in families?; sleep - plenty of it!; plants and herbs; lack of stress in the lifestyle.

(1) Your local Community Health Council has heard about these communities and asked you to produce a discussion paper about them. They want facts and evidence and have posed the following questions. Treat the questions as headings for the 4 sections of your paper. You will also need an introduction. Read through the questions and then plan how you will use the material in the passage for each one.
- Is there evidence that there are groups of people in certain communities who live much longer than the rest of us, and if so where are these communities and have they anything in common with each other?
- How long do these old people remain alert and active?
- What do scientists think are the main factors involved in such unusual longevity and are any of more importance than others, do you think?
- Can you suggest how we can use these facts in a campaign to educate the general public about living long, healthy lives and what sort of campaign might be effective?

Theme 3: Survival

In Book 3 of *Gulliver's Travels*, Jonathan Swift writes of certain people called 'Struldbruggs' who live in Luggnugg. They differ from their fellow Luggnuggians in one respect - they are immortal and never die. Their lot is not a happy one because their bodies and minds decay like normal people, so their lives become progressively more wretched. However, Gulliver did not know this at first, and his imagination was caught by the idea. Gulliver was not short of self-confidence and pride, as you will see from his ideas of what he might do were he to live for ever!

> If it had been my good fortune to come into the world a Struldbrugg, as soon as I could discover my own happiness by understanding the difference between life and death, I would first resolve by all Arts and Methods whatsoever to procure myself riches: in the pursuit of which, by thrift and management, I might reasonably expect in about two hundred years to be the wealthiest man in the kingdom. In the second place, I would from my earliest youth apply myself to the study of Arts and Sciences, by which I should arrive in time to excel all others in learning. Lastly, I would carefully record every action and event of consequence that happened in the public, impartially draw the characters of the several successions of princes and great Ministers of State; with my own observations on every point. I should exactly set down the several changes in customs, language, fashions, dress, diet and diversions. By all which acquirements, I should be a living Treasury of knowledge and wisdom, and certainly become the oracle of the nation.

2 ☆ If you were to have a guaranteed life span of 200 years during which you would retain your faculties, would your plans be anything like Gulliver's?
- Remember, you are not omnipotent, but you do have some talents which you could spend time developing.
- Make out your own life plan. Do not go into detail - you are confined to one side of A4.
- You may find it helpful to think in terms of aims for 10-year plans.

3 Organise the class in groups of 3 or 4. Each group should then exchange life plans with another group.
- Discuss the life plans your group has been given and make out an order of priority for the granting of a 200-year life-span.
- Write down your reasons for your decisions.

4 These activities will have introduced many important issues about what you feel is important in life.
- Select one such issue for a fuller treatment.
- Discuss it, and then write a brief article, suitable for a magazine, about your chosen issue.

5 Why do old people often remember their early years much more vividly than their later ones? There will be many old people in your area who remember their childhood - 50 or 60 years ago.
- Ask an old person you know to describe a typical day from their schooldays.
- You might do this individually, or you might find someone willing to visit your school and talk to the class.
- Write this up for a collection of Early Memories.

3.4 Survival in Communities.

Physical survival is one thing. But we all live in communities of one sort or another - the school, the neighbourhood, the extended family - and we have to find ways of surviving in them. It is not always easy. In future years, you will change your communities as you leave school and get a job or go away to further or higher education. You will then be in the position of being a new member of a strange community.

1 In pairs, discuss and note down what you think you would find most difficult to deal with if you were to move house tomorrow and go to a new school where you knew nobody.

When she was a child during the 1820s, Charlotte Bronte and her three sisters were sent to a boarding school for daughters of clergymen. It was a grim experience. Two of the sisters contracted tuberculosis and died. Charlotte lived to use her early school experiences in her novel, *Jane Eyre*.

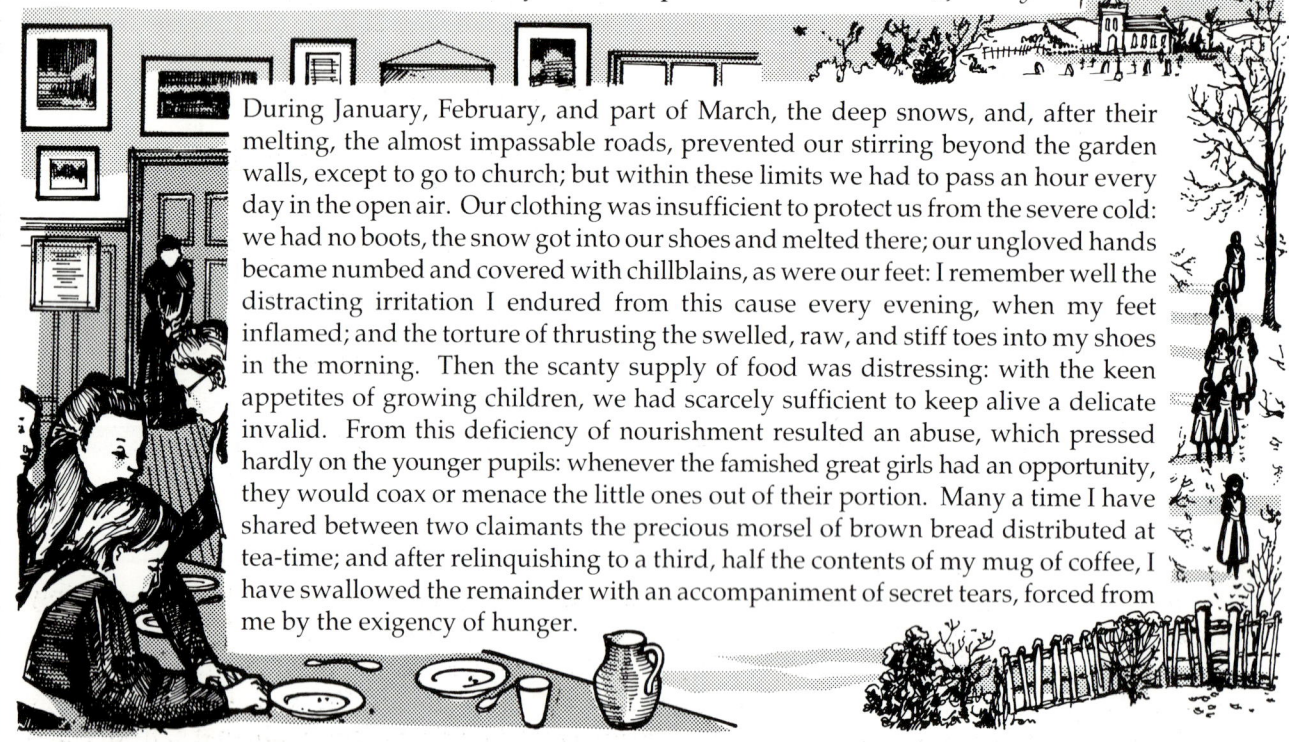

> During January, February, and part of March, the deep snows, and, after their melting, the almost impassable roads, prevented our stirring beyond the garden walls, except to go to church; but within these limits we had to pass an hour every day in the open air. Our clothing was insufficient to protect us from the severe cold: we had no boots, the snow got into our shoes and melted there; our ungloved hands became numbed and covered with chillblains, as were our feet: I remember well the distracting irritation I endured from this cause every evening, when my feet inflamed; and the torture of thrusting the swelled, raw, and stiff toes into my shoes in the morning. Then the scanty supply of food was distressing: with the keen appetites of growing children, we had scarcely sufficient to keep alive a delicate invalid. From this deficiency of nourishment resulted an abuse, which pressed hardly on the younger pupils: whenever the famished great girls had an opportunity, they would coax or menace the little ones out of their portion. Many a time I have shared between two claimants the precious morsel of brown bread distributed at tea-time; and after relinquishing to a third, half the contents of my mug of coffee, I have swallowed the remainder with an accompaniment of secret tears, forced from me by the exigency of hunger.

2 ☆ Writing letters home from such a school was a difficult task. Letters were read by the staff before being posted, and if you were too critical you would get into trouble; but you would probably want to let your parents know what it was like.
- Put yourself into the position of a young pupil and write a letter home using the material in this passage with any additions you think are appropriate.
  Although this was a girls' school, you may change it to a co-educational one for this task if you wish.

3 Exchange your letter with a neighbour and put yourself in the position of a teacher who has to censor the letter.
- Cross out anything which will make the parent think ill of the school.
- Roleplay your interview with the pupil who wrote the letter.

Theme 3: Survival

Bullying was a prominent feature of schools in the past. According to this excerpt from an article in *The Guardian*, it is still with us.

A PLACE TO GET YOUR OWN BACK IN THE BLACKBOARD JUNGLE

At last some schools are finding ways of dealing with bullies. Carla Smith sits in at a classroom court-room - inspired by Kidscape - where children decide themselves how to punish thuggish behaviour.

The infamous school bully is getting his comeuppance. Now victims can get justice by going to the school bully court where a jury, made up of school mates, will assess the problem and perhaps give an appropriate punishment.

A recent survey by the children's charity Kidscape, found that out of a group of 4,000 children aged 5 to 16, 60 per cent had been bullied seriously or repeatedly.

Persistent bullying can be terrifying and humiliating. In an attempt to help pupils help themselves, school bully courts have been introduced in about 30 English primary and secondary schools.

The courts were first suggested by a schoolgirl to Michelle Elliot, a former teacher, child psychologist and Director of Kidscape. They are usually made up of four children and a teacher. Two members are elected by the school and the other two by teachers. Each court sits for a term and is then replaced.

Both bully and victim write out their stories before the court sessions begin. Then each is questioned separately, to avoid intimidation; and they are called back, also separately, to hear the final decision.

The 30 schools with the courts understandably won't let anyone near them. So I visited a junior school in north London, which is trying out bully courts with the use of "role play".

Teacher Pat Godfrey, who has been guiding her class of eight and nine year olds through the idea for the last six months, had each group of six kids sitting round back to back tables and choosing their "bully", "victim", and four court members. They also decided the bully scenario on which the court was to pass judgment.

Here is the basis of a bullying incident.

A week ago, a fourteen-year-old (**A**) borrowed one pound from an eleven-year-old (**B**), ostensibly for a bus fare. **A** promised to return the money to **B**. Three days later, **B** asked **A** for the money. **A** said s/he had returned it and laughed at **B**. Eventually, **A** became annoyed, demanded another pound, and there was a scuffle. **B** was badly frightened and claimed s/he was hit and bruised by **A**. Four days later s/he was still so upset and worried that it might happen again that s/he decided to use the Kidscape school bully court which has just been set up in the school.

4 Write out B's version of the events. Follow this up with A's version.

5 Elect a court as explained in the article from *The Guardian*. They should sit at the front of the class. Half of the remainder of the class is A and the other half is B. With the teacher as the chairperson, question the two pupils. The court should then decide on any action to be taken.

Now try......

6 We have to face the fact that bullying exists in schools.
EITHER write a paper giving your opinions, with reasons, about what a school should do in order to deal with bullying when it occurs
OR write an account of an incident involving bullying; you may make this up or base it on a real event.

4.1 What's so Funny?

In this unit you will be thinking and reading about humour - the way its effect is achieved, and ideas about the purpose it serves.

Here are two simple cartoons of the kind you might find in a newspaper or magazine. Try to invent a caption for each one.

1. Each of these cartoons is drawn in a different style. Which style do you think is more effective?

2. The captions which originally accompanied the cartoons can be found on page 96.
   - Can you manage to invent something similar or perhaps better?
   - Do the cartoons translate easily into a verbal format?
   - Try writing a joke which can be told based on an idea in the cartoons.

3. Jokes are usually best told rather than written. In pairs try this brief experiment.
   - ✔ One person should read one of the jokes printed on page 29, then turn the page over and tell the joke.
   - ✔ The other should note down differences between the written version and the spoken version.

   Now make a list of the general differences between spoken and written language.

Theme 4: What's So Funny?

One of the ways to destroy humour is to analyse it. However, it can be interesting to reflect on why we find some things funny and not others.

A

A woman received a letter and when she read it she burst into tears.
"What's the matter?" asked her friend.
"Well, it's bad news about my nephew Sammy," said the woman. "He's got three feet."
"Three feet, surely that can't be true?" came the reply.
"Well his mother's just written to say he's grown another foot."

B

The would-be passenger rushed across the platform weighed down with suitcases and bags just in time to see his train pull out of the station. He stood there gasping and sweating when a porter said sympathetically, "Just missed your train, sir?"
"No, you idiot," fumed the man. "I didn't like the look of it so I chased it out of the station!"

C

A flute player was convinced he could use his music to tame wild animals. So he took his flute and travelled to the heart of the jungle to prove it. He had just started to play when the jungle was filled with different kinds of animals which had gathered around meekly to hear him play. There were lions, birds, tigers, hippos - animals of every kind. Just then a crocodile appeared - he had crept up from the nearby river - and gobbled up the flute player. The animals were furious.
"Why did you do that?" they cried. "We were just getting into the music."
"Eh?" said the crocodile cupping his hand to his ear.

D

A man buying a camel was told that to make it walk he should say "Few!", to make it run he should say "Many!" and to make it stop he should say "Amen!". He had his first ride. "Few!" he said and the camel started to walk.
"Many!" he cried and the camel started to run straight towards the edge of a cliff. But the man had forgotten how to make him stop. As he charged towards the cliff the man called out, "Lord save me! Amen!" Just at the edge of the cliff the camel stopped. The rider mopped his brow and said, "Phew, that was clo-AAAAAAAGH!"

4 Put these jokes (**A** to **D**) in rank order from the most to the least amusing.
- How much agreement is there in the class?
- Is there any trend in terms of preferences between boys and girls?

5 Imagine that you told one of these jokes to a friend who replied "I don't get it". Write the explanation you would give for each joke.

Now try . . . . . .

6 Make a table called *Humour - Personal Preferences* with two lists showing:
- Things I Find Funny.
- Things I Do Not Find Funny.

You can include specific names of stars, comedians and programmes as well as general items of the kind in the following list:
stand-up comedians, cartoons, knock-knock jokes, people falling over, etc.

4.2 Satire.

When we make fun of something or someone in order to highlight particular weaknesses or faults this is called "satire". It is usually (though not always) humorous and of the kind which makes you smile with recognition rather than laugh out loud. Notice that just making fun of someone, e.g. making fun of the fact that they are fat, is not satire. Making fun of their human failing, e.g. hypocrisy, vanity, is.

In the series *Fawlty Towers* the snobbishness of the hotel owner is often the object of satire. Notice how Basil's attitude changes when he finds out the identity of Melbury, a visitor to the hotel.

(Basil hurries bad-temperedly into the lobby. Melbury is standing there.)

Basil: Yes, yes, well yes?
Melbury: …Er, well, I was wondering if you could offer me accommodation for a few nights?
Basil: *(very cross)* Well, have you booked?
Melbury: … I'm sorry?
Basil: Have you booked, have you booked?
Melbury: No.
Basil: *(to himself)* Oh dear!
Melbury: Why, are you full?
Basil: Oh, we're not full… we're not full … of course we're not full!!
Melbury: I'd like, er …
Basil: One moment, one moment please …yes?
Melbury: A single room with a …
Basil: Your name, please, could I have your name?
Melbury: Melbury.

The phone rings; Basil picks it up.

Basil: *(to Melbury)* One second please. *(to phone)* Hello? … Ah, yes, Mr. O'Reilly, well it's perfectly simple. When I asked you to build me a wall I was rather hoping that instead of just dumping the bricks in a pile you might have found time to cement them together … you know, one on top of another, in the traditional fashion. *(to Melbury, testily)* Could you fill it in, please? *(to phone)* Oh, splendid! Ah, yes, but when, Mr. O'Reilly? *(to Melbury, who is having difficulty with the register)* there-there!! *(to phone)* Yes, but when? Yes, yes…ah!…the flu! *(to Melbury)* Both names, please. *(to phone)* Yes, I should have guessed, Mr. O'Reilly, that and the potato famine I suppose …
Melbury: I beg your pardon?
Basil: Would you put both your names, please?… *(to phone)* Well, will you give me a date?
Melbury: Er… I only use one.
Basil: *(with a withering look)* You don't have a first name?
Melbury: No, I am Lord Melbury, so I simply sign myself "Melbury".

There is a long, long pause.

Basil: *(to phone)* Go away. *(puts the phone down)* …I'm so sorry to have kept you waiting, your lordship … I do apologize, please forgive me. Now, was there something, is there something, anything, I can do for you? Anything at all?
Melbury: Well, I have filled this in….
Basil: Oh, please don't bother with that. *(he takes the form and throws it away)* Now, a special room? … a single? … A double? A suite? … Well, we don't have any suites, but we do have some beautiful doubles with a view …
Melbury: No, no, just a single.
Basil: Just a single! Absolutely! How very wise if I may say so, your honour.
Melbury: With a bath.
Basil: Naturally, naturally! Naturellement! *(he roars with laughter)*
Melbury: I shall be staying for one or two nights …
Basil: Oh please! Please! … Manuel!! *(he bangs the bell; nothing happens)* … Well, it's … it's rather grey today, isn't it?
Melbury: Oh, yes, it is rather.
Basil: Of course, usually down here it's quite beautiful, but today is a real old … er … rotter. *(another bang on the doorbell)* Manuel!!! … Still … it's good for the wheat.
Melbury: Yes, er, I suppose so.
Basil: Oh yes! I hear it's coming along wonderfully at

the moment! Thank God! I love the wheat ...there's no sight like a field of wheat waving in the ... waving in... Manuel!!!! *(he bangs the bell as hard as he can; no result)...* Well, how are you? I mean, if it's not a personal question. Well, it is a personal... *(he dashes from behind the desk)* Let me get your cases for you, please allow me ...
Melbury: ... Oh, thank you very much, they're just outside.
Basil: Splendid. Thank you so much. I won't be one moment ...

He sprints off, collects the cases, and returns to find Sybil talking to Lord Melbury at the counter.

Basil: ... Ah, Lord Melbury. May I introduce my wife?
Melbury: Yes, we have met.
Basil: My wife, may I introduce your lordship.
Sybil: Thank you, Basil, we've sorted it out.
Basil: Splendid, splendid.
Melbury: I wonder, could I deposit this case with you ... it's just a few valuables?
Basil: Valuables, of course. Please let me take it now. I'll put it in the safe straight away. Sybil, would you put this in the safe, please?
Sybil: I'm just off to the kitchen, Basil.
Basil: *(muttering angrily)* Yes, well, if you're too busy ...
Sybil: Nice to have met you, Lord Melbury. I hope you enjoy your stay. *(she leaves)*
Melbury: Thank you so much.
Basil: Yes, well I'll do it then, then I'll do the picture ... *(suddenly polite again)* I'll put this away in one moment, your lord. *(to Manuel, who has appeared at last)* Manuel, will you take these cases to room twenty-one.

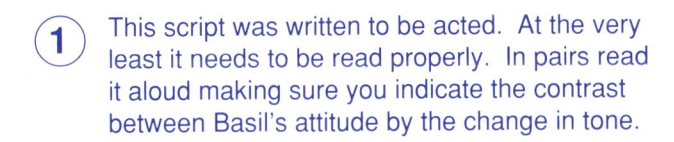

Manuel: ... Que?
Basil: Take... to room ... twenty-one. *(he surreptitiously signals the number with his fingers)*
Manuel: ...No entender.
Basil: Prenda la cacos en ... oh, doesn't matter. Right! I'll do it, I'll do it. Thank you Manuel. *(picks up the cases)*
Manuel: I take them. *(grabs cases)*
Basil: *(not letting go)* No, no, go away!
Manuel: Que? *(they struggle)*
Basil: Go and wait!
Manuel: Wait?
Basil: *(indicating the dining room)* In there! Go and wait in there! Go and be a waiter in there! *(Manuel runs off; to Melbury)* I do apologize, your lordship. I'm afraid he's only just joined us. We're training him. It'd be quicker to train a monkey, ha ha ha!

1 This script was written to be acted. At the very least it needs to be read properly. In pairs read it aloud making sure you indicate the contrast between Basil's attitude by the change in tone.

2 Write an exchange of dialogue where the reverse happens.
- Basil thinks he is addressing someone very important, e.g. a Hotel Inspector, and then finds out who he really is.
- Or try writing a scene in which a rather badly dressed couple are trying to book a room from a very snobbish hotel owner.

Now try . . . . . .

3 ☆ Write a satirical piece which makes fun of a type of person, event or place. Here are some ideas to get you thinking:
- ✔ an account of a school assembly
- ✔ school reports on famous politicians
- ✔ wanted posters for pop stars
- ✔ contrasting menus for a sophisticated restaurant and a cafe
- ✔ a speech
- ✔ an interview.

4.3 Parody.

Parody is to imitate or mimic a person's language or style for comic effect or ridicule. It is often a form of writing but need not be so; people who do impressions are often parodying their "victims". Writing a parody of an author's style can often be a way of studying the piece of writing because you have to look so closely at the way the original is constructed. In order to appreciate the parody an audience of course must know the work on which it is based.

Poem **A** is an original poem by Robert Southey written in the eighteenth century and poem **B** is a parody written by Lewis Carroll.

A

The old man's comforts and how he gained them

"You are old, Father William," the young man cried.
"The few locks which are left you are gray;
You are hale, Father William, a hearty old man,
Now tell me the reason, I pray."

"In the days of my youth," Father William replied,
"I remembered that youth would fly fast,
And abused not my health, and my vigour at first,
That I might never need them at last."

"You are old, Father William," the young man cried,
"And pleasures with youth pass away;
And yet you lament not the days that are gone,
Now tell me the reason I pray."

"In the days of my youth," Father William replied.
"I remembered that youth could not last;
I thought of the future, whatever I did,
That I never might grieve for the past."

"You are old, Father William," the young man cried,
"And life must be hastening away;
You are cheerful, and love to converse upon death,
Now tell me the reason, I pray."

"I am cheerful, young man," Father William replied,
"Let my cause thy attention engage;
In the days of my youth I remember'd my God!
And he hath not forgotten my age!"

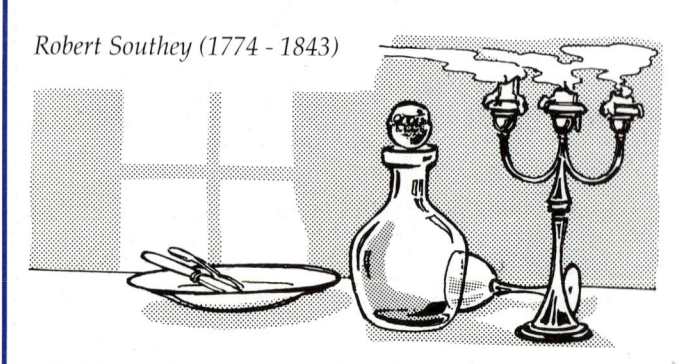

Robert Southey (1774 - 1843)

1. Notice that both poems work as a dialogue between the old and young man. In pairs take these parts and read both poems aloud trying to read each poem slightly differently - you might find that the second version is better read at a faster pace.

2. Make a list of any similarities and differences you can find between each poem, e.g.
   ✔ rhyme
   ✔ rhythm
   ✔ structure
   ✔ choice of words.
   Notice that the effectiveness of a parody depends on both the similarities and differences between the two works.

3. Why do think that Lewis Carroll chose to parody this poem?

Theme 4: What's So Funny?

B

"You are old, Father William," the young man said,
"And your hair has become very white;
And yet you incessantly stand on your head -
Do you think, at your age, it is right?"

"In my youth," Father William replied to his son,
"I feared it might injure the brain;
But, now that I'm perfectly sure I have none,
Why I do it again and again."

"You are old," said the youth, "as I mentioned before,
And have grown most uncommonly fat;
Yet you turned a back-somersault in at the door -
Pray, what is the reason of that?"

"In my youth," said the sage, as he shook his grey locks,
"I kept all my limbs very supple
By the use of this ointment - one shilling the box -
Allow me to sell you a couple?"

"You are old," said the youth, "and your jaws are too weak
For anything tougher than suet;
Yet you finished the goose, with the bones and the beak -
Pray, how did you manage to do it?"

"In my youth," said his father, "I took to the law,
And argued each case with my wife;
And the muscular strength which it gave to my jaw,
Has lasted the rest of my life."

"You are old," said the youth. "One could hardly suppose
That your eye was as steady as ever;
Yet you balanced an eel on the end of your nose -
What made you so awfully clever?"

"I have answered three questions, and that is enough,"
Said his father. "Don't give yourself airs!
Do you think I can listen all day to such stuff?
Be off, or I'll kick you down stairs!"

Lewis Carroll

Now try . . . . . .

4 Produce your own parody of a piece of writing. It could be a simple parody of a famous poem, carol or song (including pop song) or it could be a more ambitious attempt to parody the style of an author you have read. Other suggestions: tabloid newspapers, romantic love stories, adverts.

4.4 Why Do We Laugh?

1 Go through the following list (A to F) giving:
- more examples to go with each definition including, if you can, specific examples drawn from films, television or literature.
- an explanation of what the comic appeal to people might be (this is more difficult but try)

A - FARCE

This type of comedy tends to rely on ludicrous situations which develop in improbable ways; e.g. mistaken identities combined with people getting locked in rooms, losing their trousers and so on.

B - SLAPSTICK

This is comedy which involves physical action and horseplay; e.g. custard pie fights.

C - ABSURD HUMOUR

Absurd humour is exactly what the term implies - ridiculous events and situations which do not make any real logical sense. This type of humour became popular in the 1960s with programmes like *Monty Python's Flying Circus* which involved a famous sketch in which a man returns a dead parrot to a pet shop and the owner tries to convince him it is just resting.

D - BLACK HUMOUR

This type of humour deals with unpleasant aspects of life but tries to make comic situations out of them. Death, funerals, hangings can all be the subject of comedy but some people think such humour is in bad taste.

E - PRACTICAL JOKES

These can be jokes people play on each other (the book which falls when a door opens, flowers which squirt water, whoopee cushions, etc) but they can also be the subject of television programmes in which people are fooled in elaborate ways.

F - VERBAL HUMOUR

Puns are perhaps the most common form of verbal humour - they rely on ambiguities of meaning and the fact that words can sound the same but mean something different.

Theme 4: What's So Funny?

Various writers have offered explanations for the purposes served by humour and laughter. Here are some of them. No explanation is totally convincing but they all seem to have some element of truth.

1. LAUGHTER IS AN EXPRESSION OF SUPERIORITY

If you think about it many jokes and funny situations seem to rely on either a person's lack of understanding or their misfortune. The sight of someone slipping on a banana skin or falling off a chair can often cause laughter.

2. LAUGHTER IS ACTUALLY AN EXPRESSION OF AGGRESSION

Humour is a way of expressing aggression in a safe way which is accepted by society. Some people have claimed that the actual physical act of laughing has its origins in the animal practice of baring teeth. Many jokes are made at the expense of people who are in superior positions we want to somehow "get at" in a safe, unhurtful way.

3. LAUGHTER IS A DEFENCE AGAINST REALITY

The idea here is that humour is a way of protecting ourselves from painful or hurtful situations. It is interesting the way a disaster can produce a spate of jokes. How do we explain the phenomenon of "sick" jokes? Some people have been known to joke when they have been facing death by execution.

4. LAUGHTER IS A RELEASE FROM STRESS OR STRAIN

Laughter is supposed to be physically good for you. People will often say "I needed a good laugh". When a social situation is a bit awkward or strained the ice can be broken by some situation which makes everyone laugh. However laughter can also be a sign of stress - especially when people laugh at things that do not seem to be that funny.

2 Comment on each of these explanations (1 - 4) saying whether it seems to be true and giving examples of situations which seem to confirm what is being said. You could refer to the types of humour listed on page 34.

3 The context often determines whether something is funny or not.
- ✔ Someone falling off a chair is not that funny; if it happens in the middle of a solemn occasion it is.
- ✔ A man with his shirt hanging out is not particularly funny but if he is giving a lecture to a large group of people then perhaps it is. It will be even funnier if he is behaving in a pompous way.
- • Think of a situation you have been in where you have found something very funny and describe not just what happened but why it was so amusing.

Now try . . . . . .

4 In groups choose a project which will result in a presentation to the rest of the class. Some suggestions:
- a sequence of mock adverts
- a reading from a comedy play
- a "take off" of a television game show
- a sketch of some kind
- a presentation about the whole subject of humour and comedy.

5.1 In the News.

In this unit you will be studying the media - television, newspapers and the radio. You will also be taking a look at the world of advertising.

How much do you know about what is going on in the world?

1 In groups of 3 or 4, discuss and write down:
- ✔ what you think are the 6 most important news stories at the moment
- ✔ how you learned about the news stories
- ✔ which radio stations, daily newspapers and television programmes you get most of your news from.

Compare lists, try to explain differences and present your findings on one sheet of paper.

2 Suppose you work as a presenter on a local radio station. One of your daily tasks is to give 3 minute news broadcasts. You have been given the stories illustrated on this page.
Prepare your news broadcast, working through the following stages:
- ✓ Work out how many words you speak in 1 minute when reading them out clearly. Multiply by 3 to find how many words you need for your broadcast. Choose the order in which to present the stories; you may not have time for them all.
- ✓ Write the script for each story. All the details you might want to use are not necessarily here, so add your own ideas.
- ✓ Try out your broadcast. Use a tape-recorder or deliver it to the class.
- ✓ Did you all choose the same lead story?
- ✓ What differences in presentation were there?

SERIOUS CAR CRASH
M4 near Reading - 2 killed, 20 plus injured. Police say speeding to blame.

THREE-YEAR-OLD KAREN LOCAL HEART-TRANSPLANT PATIENT - DOING WELL.

Prime Minister says striking teachers should return to work.

H.M.I. REPORT CRITICISES LOCAL SCHOOL.
Parents call for action.

RUSSIA AND FRANCE SIGN FAR-REACHING TRADE AGREEMENT.
Britain's reaction - it's a threat to the E.E.C..

LOCAL SUPERMARKET FIRE. NO-ONE HURT. ARSON SUSPECTED. BUILDING GUTTED.

Local girl Tania Stearman chosen to represent Great Britain at chess.

GOVERNMENT WARNING INFLATION WILL RISE IN NEXT FEW MONTHS WILL FALL LATER.

BRITISH ATHLETE KIM ROBERTS BREAKS WORLD RECORD FOR 1500 METRES CALIFORNIA - BRITAIN - U.S. COMPETITION.

Now try......

3 Having listened to others, and discussed your broadcasts, you are in a very good position to give advice to others. Write down 6 pieces of advice for future radio news presenters.

Theme 5: In the News

WHAT TELEVISION PROGRAMMES DO YOU WATCH?

4 Keep a television viewing diary for 1 week in which you note down all the programmes you watch.
- Compare diaries.
- List television programmes or types of programme (e.g. football matches), that you regularly watch, under the headings as in A.

5 Select one programme from your highest category and write a newspaper review of it. You must keep two reader audiences in mind:
- ✔ People who have seen the programme and want to know what someone else thought of it.
- ✔ People who haven't seen the programme but want to find out about it because they might watch a repeat or further episodes.

A

I never miss if I can help it	I enjoy	I watch if I've nothing better to do
'Neighbours'	'Blind Date'	'Eastenders'
Show jumping	Cartoons	News
'The Generation Game'	'Sesame Street'	'Bread'
'That's Life'	'The Bill'	'Blue Peter'
'Coronation Street'	'Home and Away'	
'The Golden Girls'	Athletics	
	Wildlife Programmes	
	Game Shows	

Emily M.

'That's Life' has been a popular T.V. programme for many years. It deals with issues like Child Abuse, and the serious effects of drinking and driving, and they tell you about 'rip-off merchants'. I think this programme is good because even when they are handling the most delicate matters they do it with tact and understanding.

6 In pairs, discuss and make notes on what each of your 2 audiences wants to read about in your review.
- List a series of questions for each audience.
- Make notes about your chosen programme to answer those questions.
- Finally, write out your review.

Now try . . . . . .

7 Take a review of a television programme from any newspaper or magazine and test it against your notes about what audiences are looking for. Does the review answer any other questions which you didn't think to ask?

5.2 Different Versions.

1. In pairs, write up the incident depicted above. You are freelance journalists; this means that you are not employed by one newspaper, but you sell your stories to any newspaper that will buy them. This time, you have decided to write 2 articles about the incident, for 2 very different papers.
   - Select the 2 newspapers for which you are writing.
   - Research into what sort of articles those newspapers publish. You will need to read several articles from each paper and make notes about the styles.
   - Decide who will write the first draft for each paper - 1 each.
   - Write the first drafts.
   - Swop your drafts, and edit each other's articles. Be ruthless - editors are! Make clear what changes are needed.
   - Return drafts to each other and write final versions.

Theme 5: In the News

QUESTIONS OF MORALITY

Is it right that reporters should harass people in order to get stories? **A** is NOT a true story. All the facts, people, and the hospital are fictitious, but it should give you a case to discuss.

A

THE FOURWINDS HOSPITAL STORY - THE FACTS

On 6 May, Mrs Joanne Smethwick gave birth to a baby boy at Fourwinds Private Maternity Hospital. On 8 May, the baby developed an illness which remained undiagnosed until too late. The baby died on the morning of May 10.

Mrs Smethwick returned home immediately and naturally she and her husband were distraught; they refused to talk to any reporters. The hospital released only the basic facts and refused to give any more details or to discuss possible causes of the tragedy; they said any details would have to wait until after the inquest.

A local freelance reporter, James Medwin, became suspicious. He posed as a Health official and managed to get into Mr and Mrs Smethwick's home to question them before they realised who he was. By the time he left, Mrs Smethwick was hysterical and her husband was only stopped from assaulting James Medwin by the need to phone their doctor immediately.

But, as a result of his persistence, James Medwin had picked up the fact that evidence pointed to a virus as the cause of the death. The hospital refused him an interview, so the next night he broke into the office and found evidence which pointed to a virus, located in the hospital, being the cause. He immediately wrote the story up, and was able to sell it locally and to the national press. By doing this and giving media interviews, James Medwin made a lot of money. The hospital was forced to close immediately because once the patients were aware of the possible danger they refused to stay; the owners were ruined financially.

The inquest confirmed that, essentially, James Medwin had been right, although it would have been possible for the hospital to have contained the outbreak with very little risk to any babies, had they been given the chance.

2 Use the following as points for a discussion of A:
- Whose interests was James Medwin serving?
- ☆ Do you think he was right in every case to do what he did?
- Were there alternative courses of action open to him which would have been just as effective in preventing more deaths? If so, why didn't he take them?
- Did the hospital authorities behave correctly?
- Do we need a financial motive in order to preserve the freedom of the press to investigate matters of public interest?
- Was the hospital an unavoidable casualty of the need to frighten people away from it?
- Did people HAVE to be frightened away?
- Do you admire James Medwin, or have you other opinions of him?

Now try . . . . . .

3 When you have come to some conclusions about the issues raised in A, write a newspaper article, headed: *The Fourwinds Hospital Story: Moral Issues.*

5.3 Presenting News.

QUESTION: Are facts and opinions always kept separate in newspapers?
QUESTION: Is it always obvious which is fact and which is opinion in newspapers?
QUESTION: Where, particularly, would you look in a newspaper for expression of opinions?

WHAT IS IN A NEWSPAPER?

① For this activity you need to be in groups of about 3 people and each group will need a copy of a different newspaper - all published on the same day. When you have a good spread of types of papers, you can make an analysis of a newspaper. All newspapers contain the following:
- ✓ News stories
- ✓ Sports news
- ✓ Pictures
- ✓ Opinion
- ✓ Advertisements
- ✓ Letters
- ✓ Television and radio
- ✓ Cartoons/strip cartoons
- ✓ Personal announcements

Some newspapers contain other features such as crosswords, astrology forecasts, and even short stories. Put anything that does not fit easily under the above 9 headings under a tenth:
- ✓ Miscellaneous.

Theme 5: In the News

You will need a rough way of estimating HOW MUCH there is of each of these. A lot of your material will be spread across several pages, so the easiest measure to use is COLUMN CENTIMETRES. Of course, not every column is the same width as every other column, but this will give you a unit accurate enough for your purpose. You will, therefore, need to measure each piece of the newspaper and keep a running score of column centimetres under each of the headings.

② When you have collected all the measurements, make a display of the facts about your newspaper on one side of A4. This can be displayed together with those from other groups to reach conclusions about:
- ✔ which newspaper analysed in this way represents the best value for money
- ✔ which you would choose to read and why.

③ Take a major news story and collect at least 3 versions of it from different newspapers. Discuss in small groups how the 3 versions differ and make notes about the differences. You will need to look at:
- headlines
- details included or omitted
- details emphasised
- choice of words
- opinions expressed.

Can you make any generalisations about the different newspapers and their views?

41

5.4 Fair and honest?

> "Advertisement" means any form of representation which is made in connection with a trade, business, craft or profession in order to promote the supply or transfer of goods or sevices, immovable property, rights or obligations. For the purposes of these Regulations an advertisement is misleading if in any way, including its presentation, it deceives or is likely to deceive the persons to whom it is addressed or whom it reaches and if, by reason of its deceptive nature, it is likely to affect their economic behaviour or, for those reasons, injures or is likely to injure a competitor of the person whose interests the advertisement seeks to promote.

Extract from Regulation 2 of the Control of Misleading Advertisements Regulations, 1988.

IF AN ADVERT IS WRONG, WHO PUTS IT RIGHT?

We do. The Advertising Standards Authority ensures advertisements meet with the strict Code of Advertising Practice. So if you question an advertiser, they have to answer to us.

To find out more about the ASA, please write to Advertising Standards Authority, Department X, Brook House, Torrington Place, London WC1E 7HN.

ASA

This space is donated in the interests of high standards in advertisements.

Our national laws are defined - some would say obscured - in such language of officialese. Notice the number of phrases in parenthesis. You should be able to express the passage simply and more concisely.

Perhaps the most common ways in which an advertisement can mislead are as follows:

- ✓ if it contains a false statement of fact;
- ✓ if it conceals or leaves out important facts;
- ✓ if it promises to do something but there is no intention of carrying out the promise.

If an advertisement is guilty of one of these, then the advertisers may be prosecuted; more likely, they would be warned and the advertisement withdrawn.

Advertisements go very close to these lines without actually crossing them. They do so mainly to try to persuade you and me to part with our money. So it is in our interests to understand how advertisements work and what they are trying to do.

Advertisements are continually replaced by more up-to-date ones; so there aren't any in this, book for you to work on. Instead, choose a recent one for yourself from a newspaper or magazine. It should have enough in it to make it worth analysing.

① Analyse an advertisement. Use the following questions and any more of your own that are relevant to your advertisement. Write up your analysis as a report with a series of statements answering the questions followed by a paragraph in which you judge the advertisement.

- What is the advertisement trying to sell?
- To whom is it directed? (Be exact. For example, "Balding, middle-aged men".)
- Pick out any key words emphasised by the advertisement. What impressions are they intended to give?
- If there are any pictures, are they realistic?
- Does the advertisement play on any fears?
- Does the advertisement give precise information or vague impressions?
- What arguments does the advertisement use?
- Does the advertisement assume a particular kind of lifestyle, and if so, what is it?
- Does the advertisement come close to offending against any of the three common ways of misleading?
- Is the advertisement effective AND fair?

Theme 5: In the News

EGGLESCLIFFE ENTERPRISE
29 Nov

Poly's in North East Threaten to Strike

By S.Phillips

Lecturers in the North-East threaten to esculate their industrial dispute amid reports of "secret talks" between polys bosses and their national negotiator.

The row broke out negotiations which polyte north believe are doomed

They are already pla week and are voting on a administrative duties ban

Union laeder John a sceret meeting with and Colleages Empl executive,took place in although Mr Ward deni that day.

Bosses at Newcastle,Sund Teesside polytechnics agreed they routine regional meeting but no P.C.E.F. was present.

Insisting his information was result of this meetin bend any lecturer wh action.

attempt to suspend me ial industrial action sculation of the dispu Newcastle assistant d There is no question c ut pay, but if s will be withheld acco te."

Hospit

There was a televi German television mad Kohl. He asked Ger money and food to th Soviet Union.The dist children waiting in qu

Dog ru

Mr Mallon who is an art teacher at Egglescliffe school did the Great North Run in Newcastle to raise money for the Guide Dogs. Mr Mallon has done the run for 10 years and enjoys it very much. He raised money for the Blind because it is a single charity and is local, also because he appreciates his sight and would not know what to do without it.

It took him 1 hour 37 minutes on the 16th September. over 530 people sponsored him. Mr Mallon was very pleased and thats what made him keep going. In the end he raised enough money to buy a Guide Dog for the blind.

children waiting in queues to be served for food accompanied his broadcast.

Weather

There will be another frosty night and foggy start over most of the country with light wind.

The south east will start cloudy with little rain but this should move away during the morning. As fog lifts most areas will become dry with some sunny periods. But it will not be particularly warm

r Oliv

Tuesday 27th Novem with our own dear l facts unknown befor hool pupils. For insta nterests at heart as h honey he'd like to pool and a dry ski e'd also like to as pitch (astro turf is hen asked about what, as that he had ho walking and windsurfing. Als wanted to have a go at hang-g

Mr. Oliver has two childre lives in London and a s Newcastle he was born in Yo than be a teacher he woul Yorkshire cricket team but fo didn't have enough talent.

When he first came to thi becoming head teacher, whil the hall, the brass band was He now considers this his he got the job.

---

② PUTTING A NEWSPAPER TOGETHER
Or, in your case, the first page only.
- Work in groups of 4 or 5. Appoint an overall editor.
- You will need a large sheet of paper, scissors and glue, as well as writing materials.
- Stick your material on to the large sheet. In this way you will be able to try different overall designs before deciding on exactly how it will look.

A suggested way of proceeding.
✔ Decide on the context for your newspaper. It could be based on current national and international news, or you might try a local School News issue. Plan to include advertisements and pictures as well. Are you going to use colour? What are you going to call it?
✔ Share out the tasks.
✔ Write your drafts.
✔ Pass the drafts to the editor for editing.
✔ Write your final versions.
✔ Proofread each other's final versions and make any necessary corrections.
✔ Put it all together as the front page of a newspaper for wall display.

6.1 What's Your Opinion?

In this unit you will be considering controversial issues, doing some research, interpreting a story, and listening and contributing to discussions.

Do you agree or disagree with the statements shown in **A**? Note down your opinion on each one. Then discuss them with your neighbour and see if you can agree in each case. Lastly, find out, by a show of hands, what the class thinks.

A

Placards read:
- MEDICAL EXPERIMENTS ON LIVING ANIMALS SHOULD BE BANNED
- SCHOOL LEAVING AGE SHOULD BE LOWERED TO 14
- YOU ARE NOT ENTITLED TO AN OPINION UNLESS YOU KNOW THE SUBJECT VERY WELL.
- IT SHOULD BE ILLEGAL TO SELL DRINKS IN CANS, THEY SHOULD BE IN RETURNABLE BOTTLES AND DEPOSIT PAID.
- IT IS NEVER JUSTIFIABLE TO BREAK THE LAW WHEN YOU ARE CAMPAIGNING HOWEVER WORTHY THE CAUSE.

REMINDER - Discussions.

It is no bad thing to change your mind as a result of hearing new evidence or because of a powerful argument. Everybody enjoys a good discussion. But in order to have a good discussion, you need to:
- ✓ know enough about the subject;
- ✓ be willing to listen to other people's opinions;
- ✓ be prepared to make your contribution.

Most of us know someone who omits the first two!

☆ GENDER ISSUES

A school English adviser once wrote the following about schools she had seen.

We went to look at the reception class. The boys were playing with construction bricks. The girls had aprons on and were washing dolls' clothes in a tub.

The same issue arose in a secondary school inspection recently. In the option choices no girls did Physics AND Chemistry and the proportion of girls to boys in Physics groups was one in five. In this same school, the staff were waited on at lunchtime by girls and the coffee served by girls.

Tape-recordings made by teachers for in-service work of small group discussions followed a recognisable pattern. When the group is mixed-sex, the boys disrupt.

There are Comprehensive Schools where 17 men hold senior positions and only Home Economics and Remedial Departments have female Heads.

In one school a very experienced female was not short-listed for a Head of Department post because the Head wanted a man, the reason given being that the Department was all female.

44

Theme 6: What's Your Opinion?

None of this is new. It has been documented over and over again, this apparent circle of learned and re-inforced stereotypes. The children enter school with their gender roles ascribed and learned and the curriculum and staffing structures, indeed all the minutiae of the school day, endorse how they are.
It is now accepted that boys and girls should have access to the same opportunities at school and afterwards. But in practice this is not always true, and it can work against both boys and girls.

1 These questions are for discussion. Make notes about them first; then discuss them in pairs; lastly, find out what the class thinks.
- ✓ Why do you think the authors chose the following titles for two books about sexism in children's lives?
  "Boys don't cry" and
  "Pour out the cocoa, Janet".
- ✓ The English adviser was writing about schools some years ago. But some things in our society change very slowly. Look at each of her paragraphs in turn. Has your school experience been like that?
- ✓ One of the reasons for the slow change is that "children enter school with their gender roles ascribed and learned". What exactly does this mean?
  Is it wholly a bad thing?
  How could it, realistically, be changed?
- ✓ Do you think children should be educated in co-educational or single sex schools? Does your opinion change with the age - or sex - of the child?
- ✓ If yours is a single sex school, in what ways do you think it gives you MORE opportunities than would be the case in a co-educational school, and in what ways does it LIMIT your opportunities?
- ✓ If yours is a co-educational school, investigate it in terms of how it deals with boys and girls.
  How fair is it?

2 Gender issues are difficult - and controversial - so you might approach them using some or all of the following stages. You will find that some of you notice things that others do not; this is the nature of this issue and the reason why it needs discussion together.
- Note down anything that has happened to you recently in school which would have been different were you of the other sex.
- Keep a SELECTIVE diary for one day. If you are in a single sex school note down every occasion when you would have been treated differently had the other sex been present; if you are in a co-educational school, note down every occasion when boys and girls were treated differently. It is important that you should NOT judge whether it mattered or not at this stage; just make a note of it.
- Interview a teacher to find out what are their opinions on gender issues in school.
- Share your experiences and impressions in small groups. Report back to the whole class on any matters which you have identified as important.

Now try . . . . . .

3 You could take this further by making a wall display about the subject. You could get more material from the Equal Opportunities Commission.

45

6.2 The Flute Player.

Some stories do not have much action in them, but are worth reading for other reasons. *The Flute Player* by Ruskin Bond is one of these. It is a story with several themes, not all obvious at first reading.

Down the main road passed big yellow buses, cars, ponydrawn tongas, motorcycles and bullock-carts. This steady flow of traffic seemed, somehow, to form a barrier between the city on one side of the trunk road, and the distant sleepy villages on the other. It seemed to cut India in half - the India Kamla knew slightly, and the India she had never seen.

Kamla's grandmother lived on the outskirts of the city of Jaipur; just across the road from the house there were fields and villages stretching away for hundreds of miles. Kamla had never been across the main road which separated the busy city from the flat green plains stretching endlessly towards the horizon.

Kamla was used to city life. In England, it was London and Manchester. In India, it was Delhi and Jaipur. Rainy Manchester was, of course, different in many ways from sun-drenched Jaipur, and Indian cities had stronger smells and more vibrant colours than their English counterparts. Nevertheless, they had much in common: busy people always on the move, money constantly changing hands, buses to catch, schools to attend, parties to attend, TV to watch. Kamla had seen very little of the English countryside, even less of India outside the cities.

Her parents lived in Manchester, where her father was a doctor in a large hospital. She went to school in England. But this year, during the summer holidays, she had come to India to stay with her grandmother. Apart from a maidservant and a grizzled old night-watchman, Grandmother lived quite alone, in a small house on the outskirts of Jaipur. During the winter months, Jaipur's climate was cool and bracing; but in the summer, a fierce sun poured down upon the city from a cloudless sky.

None of the other city children ventured across the main road into the fields of millet, wheat and cotton, but Kamla was determined to visit the fields before she returned to England. From the flat roof of the house she could see them stretching away for miles, the ripening wheat swaying in the hot wind. Finally, when there were only two days left before she went to Delhi to board a plane for London, she made up her mind and crossed the main road.

She did this in the afternoon, when Grandmother was asleep and the servants were in the bazaar. She slipped out of the back door, and her slippers kicked up the dust as she ran down the path to the main road. A bus roared past, and more dust rose from the road and swirled about her. Kamla ran through the dust, past the jacaranda trees that lined the road, and into the fields.

Suddenly the world became an enormous place, bigger and more varied than it seemed from the air; mysterious and exciting - and a little frightening.

The sea of wheat stretched away till it merged with the hot blinding blue of the sky. Far to her left were a few trees and the low white huts of the village. To her right lay hollow pits of red dust and a hollowed chimney, where bricks used to be made. In front, some distance away, Kamla could see a camel moving round a well, drawing up water for the fields. She set out in the direction of the camel.

Her grandmother had told her not to wander on her own in the city; but this wasn't the city, and as far as she knew, camels did not attack people.

It took her a long time to get to the camel. It was about half a mile away, though it seemed much nearer. And when Kamla reached it, she was surprised to find out that there was no one else in sight. The camel was turning the wheel by itself, moving round and round the well, while the water kept gushing up in little trays to come down the channels into the fields. The camel took no notice of Kamla, did not look at her even once, just carried on about its business.

There must be someone here thought Kamla, walking towards a mango tree a few yards away. Ripe mangoes dangled like globules of gold from its branches. Under the tree, fast asleep, was a boy.

All he wore was a pair of dirty white shorts. His body had been burnt dark with the sun; his hair was tussled, his feet chalky with dust. In the palm of his outstretched hand was a flute. He was a thin boy, with long bony legs, but Kamla felt that he was strong too, for his body was hard and wiry.

Kamla came nearer to the sleeping boy, peering at him with some curiosity, for she had not seen a village boy before. Her shadow fell across his face. The coming of the shadow woke the boy. He opened his eyes and stared at Kamla. When she did not say anything, he sat up, his head a little to one side, his hands clasping his knees, and stared at her.

"Who are you?" he asked a little gruffly. He was not used to waking up and finding strange girls staring at him.

"I'm Kamla. I've come from England, but I'm really from India. I mean I've come home to India, but I'm really from England." This was getting to be

Theme 6: What's Your Opinion?

rather confusing, so she countered with an abrupt: "Who are you?"

"I'm the strongest boy in the village," said the boy, deciding to assert himself without any more ado. "My name is Romi. I can wrestle and swim and climb any tree."

"And do you sleep a lot?" asked Kamla innocently. Romi scratched his head and grinned.

"I must look after the camel," he said. "It is no use staying awake for the camel. It keeps on going around the well until it is tired, and then it stops. When it has rested, it starts going around again. It can carry on like that all day. But it eats a lot."

Mention of the camel's food reminded Romi that he was hungry. He was growing fast these days, and was nearly always hungry. There were some mangoes lying beside him, and he offered one to Kamla. They were silent for a few minutes. You cannot suck mangoes and talk at the same time. After they had finished, they washed their hands in the water from one of the trays.

"There are parrots in the tree," said Kamla, noticing three or four parrots conducting a noisy meeting in the topmost branches. They reminded her a bit of a pop group she had seen and heard back home.

"They spoilt most of the mangoes," said Romi. He flung a stone at them, missing, but they took off with squawks of protest, flashes of green and gold wheeling in the sunshine.

"Where do you swim?" asked Kamla. "Down in the well?"

"Of course not, I'm not a frog. There is a canal not far from here. Come, I will show you!"

As they crossed the fields, a pair of blue-jays flew out of a bush, rockets of bright blue that dipped and swerved, rising and swerving and falling as they chased each other.

Remembering a story that Grandmother had told her, Kamla said, "They are sacred birds, aren't they? Because of their blue throats." She told him of the story of the god Shiva having a blue throat because he had swallowed a poison that would have destroyed the world; he had kept the poison in his throat and would not let it go further. "And so his throat is blue, like the blue-jay's."

Romi liked this story. His respect for Kamla was greatly increased. But he was not to be outdone, and when a small grey squirrel dashed across the path he told her that squirrels, too, were sacred. Krishna, the god who had been born into a farmer's family like Romi's, had been fond of squirrels and would take them in his arms and stroke them.

"That is why squirrels have four dark lines down their backs." said Romi. "Krishna was as dark as I am, and the stripes are the marks of his fingers."

"Can you catch a squirrel?" asked Kamla.

"No, they are too quick. But I caught a snake once. I caught it by its tail and dropped it in the well. That well is full of snakes. Whenever we catch one, instead of killing it, we drop it in the well! They can't get out."

Kamla shuddered at the thought of all those snakes swimming and wriggling about at the bottom of the deep well. She wasn't sure that she wanted to return to the well with him. But she forgot about the snakes when they reached the canal.

It was a small canal, about ten metres wide, and only waist-deep in the middle, but it was very muddy at the bottom. She had never seen such a muddy stream in all her life.

"Would you like to get in?" asked Romi.

"No," said Kamla. "You get in."

Romi was only too ready to show off his tricks in the water. His toes took a firm hold on the grassy bank, the muscles of his calves tensed, and he dived into the water with a loud splash, landing rather awkwardly on his belly. It was a poor dive but Kamla was impressed.

Romi swam across to the opposite bank and then back again. When he climbed out of the water, he was covered with mud. It made him look quite fierce. "Come on in," he invited. "It's not deep."

"It's dirty," said Kamla, but she felt tempted too.

"It's only mud," said Romi. "There's nothing wrong with mud. Camels and buffaloes love mud."

"I'm not a camel - or a buffalo."

"All right. You don't have to go right in. Just walk along the sides of the channel."

After a moment's hesitation, Kamla slipped her feet out of her slippers, and crept cautiously down the slope till her feet were in the water. She went no further, but even so, some of the muddy water splashed on to her clean white skirt. What would she tell her Grandmother? Her feet sank into the soft mud, and she gave a little squeal as the water reached her knees. It was with some difficulty that she got each foot out of the sticky mud.

Romi took her by the hand, and they went stumbling along the side of the channel while little fish swam in and out of their legs, and a heron, one foot raised, waited until they had passed before snapping a fish out of the water. The little fish glistened in the sun before it disappeared down the heron's throat.

Romi gave a sudden exclamation and then came to a stop. Kamla held onto him for support.

"What is it?" she asked, a little nervously.

"It's a tortoise," said Romi. "Can you see it?"

The Flute Player

He pointed to the bank of the canal, and there, lying quite still, was a small tortoise. Romi scrambled up the bank and, before Kamla could stop him, had picked up the tortoise. As soon as he touched it, the animal's head and legs disappeared into its shell. Romi turned it over, but from behind the breast-plate only the head and the spiky tail were visible.

"Look!" exclaimed Kamla, pointing to the ground where the tortoise was lying. "What's in that hole?"

They peered into the hole. It was about half a metre deep, and at the bottom were about five or six white eggs, a little smaller than a hen's eggs.

"Put it back," said Kamla. "It was sitting on its eggs."

Romi shrugged and dropped the tortoise back on its hole. It peeped out from behind its shell, saw the children still present, and retreated into its shell.

"I must go," said Kamla. "It's getting late. Granny will wonder where I have gone."

They walked back to the mango tree, and washed their hands and feet in the cool clear water of the well; but only after Romi had assured Kamla that there weren't any snakes in the well - he had been talking about an old disused well on the far side of the village. Kamla told Romi she would take him to her house one day, but it would have to be next year, or perhaps the year after, when she came to India again.

"Is it very far, where are you going?" asked Romi.

"Yes, England is across the seas. I have to go back to my parents. And my school is there, too. I will take the plane from Delhi. Have you ever been there?"

"I have not been further than Jaipur," said Romi.

"What is England like? Are there canals to swim in?"

"You can swim in the sea. Lots of people go swimming in the sea. But it's too cold most of the year. Where I live, there are shops and cinemas and places where you can eat anything. People from all over the world come to live there. You can see red faces, brown faces, black faces, white faces!"

"I saw a red face once," said Romi. "He came to the village to take pictures. He took one of me sitting on the camel. He said he would send me the picture, but it never came."

Kamla noticed the flute lying on the grass. "Is it your flute?," she asked.

"Yes," said Romi. "It is an old flute. But the old ones are best. I found it lying in a field last year. Perhaps it was the god Krishna's! He was always playing the flute."

"And who taught you to play it?"

"I learnt by myself. Shall I play it for you?"

Kamla nodded, and they sat down on the grass, leaning against the trunk of the mango tree, and Romi put the flute to his lips and began to play.

It was a slow, sweet tune, a little sad, a little happy, and the notes were taken up by the breeze and carried across the fields. There was no one to hear the music except the birds and the camel and Kamla. Whether the camel liked it or not, we shall never know; it just kept going round and round the well, drawing up water for the fields. And whether the birds liked it or not, we cannot say, although it is true that they were suddenly silent when Romi began to play. But Kamla was charmed by the music, and she watched Romi while he played, and the boy smiled at her with his eyes and ran his fingers along the flute. When he stopped playing, everything was still, everything silent, except for the soft wind sighing in the wheat and the gurgle of water coming up from the well.

Kamla stood up to leave.

"When will you come again?" asked Romi.

"I will try to come next year," said Kamla.

"That is a long time. By then you will be quite old. You may not want to come."

"I will come," said Kamla.

"Promise?"

"Promise."

Romi put the flute in her hands and said, "You keep it. I can get another one."

"But I don't know how to play it," said Kamla.

"It will play by itself," said Romi.

She took the flute and put it to her lips and blew on it, producing a squeaky little note that startled a lone parrot out of the mango tree. Romi laughed, and while he was laughing, Kamla turned and ran down the path through the fields. When she had gone some distance she turned and waved to Romi with the flute. He stood near the well and waved back.

Cupping his hands to his mouth, he shouted across the fields: "Don't forget to come next year!"

And Kamla turned back, "I won't forget." But her voice was faint, and the breeze blew the words away and Romi did not hear them.

Was England home? wondered Kamla. Or was this Indian city home? Or was her true home in that other India, across the busy trunk road? Perhaps she would find out one day.

Romi watched her until she was just a speck in the distance, and then he turned and shouted at the camel, telling it to move faster. But the camel did not even glance at him, it just carried on as before, as India had carried on for hundreds of years, round and round the well, while the water gurgled and splashed over the smooth stones.

Theme 6: What's Your Opinion?

There are no "right" answers in the interpretation of a story, but plenty of chances to discuss informed opinions.

1 Select one of the themes (A to D), all of which run through the story. Make notes about every occasion when your chosen theme is present. Make sure that all four themes are covered in the class.

- ✓ **Theme A** Kamla undergoing new experiences.
- ✓ **Theme B** The developing relationship between the girl and the boy.
- ✓ **Theme C** Contrasts between things and between people.
- ✓ **Theme D** People's roots and belonging to a culture.

Example. **Theme C** 1. Indian city life is a contrasted with Indian country life and the road seems to be a barrier.

☆ **SYMBOLISM**

We use symbols all the time in our society. Uniforms are symbols, but they do not necessarily mean the same thing to everyone. A school uniform to one person may be a welcome symbol that they belong to a society, whereas to another it may be an unwelcome symbol of control by that society. Writers use symbols, consciously and unconsciously.

4 In the story, what might be the possible significance behind the following apart from their literal meanings?
- The flute.
- "And Kamla called back, 'I won't forget.' But her voice was faint, and the breeze blew the words away and Romi did not hear them."
- The camel.

2 Look through your notes and try to see them as a path through the story. Between you, there will then be four "paths" showing how the story develops.
- Share your ideas about these four paths.
- How much overlap is there?
- Which path do you think is the most important and why?
- Can you find a way of representing the four paths together diagrammatically?

3 Take any one of these themes or paths and write your own story with that idea at the heart of it.

Our society contains many contrasts: rich - poor; north - south; black - white; the different cultures and religions; people whose ancestors have lived in the same place for generations and those who have moved in recently, either from other parts of the country or from abroad. The multi-cultural mix in Britain contains all these - and more. Such a mixture makes our society much more interesting, but differences can also lead to problems when people are discriminated against just because they are different in some way. This happens to all of us sometimes, and to some of us more than others.

5 Think back to something that happened to you because you were singled out in some way. It could be because of where you live, your colour, your dress, your opinion, your religion, or anything at all.
- Write down what happened.
- Write down what you think could be done to stop this happening in the future.

Now try . . . . . .

6 Take one general issue that has been raised by these particular incidents and discuss it from the point of view of the people who are singled out. Be careful to work towards understanding - not towards a judgment.

6.3 A Formal Debate.

In order to allow a group of people to manage anything from a society to an entire country mankind has developed a system of debating with formal rules. These are more or less complicated according to need, but all are based on one simple premiss: the discussion is controlled by one person who is responsible for ensuring that everyone gets a fair chance to argue his or her case.

That is a challenge, bearing in mind how strongly people feel about controversial issues, and how many people want to express their opinions all at the same time. Clearly there is a need for a system which is fair to everyone, and to which everyone agrees to conform. That is what a formal debate is intended to ensure. It demands self-discipline from everyone involved.

This section is intended to help you to achieve such a debate in your class.

RULES

- The Chair controls the debate; whatever s/he says must be observed.
- Everyone else must address all their remarks to the Chair.

PRINCIPLES

First, you have to accept, and keep to, two principles.
- Whoever is in the Chair is in charge and their orders must be obeyed.
- Everyone is entitled to be given a hearing, however much you may disagree with some of the views expressed.

PROCEDURE

- The Chair will introduce the subject for debate (the Motion) and will then call on each speaker in turn.
- The order of speaking will be as follows:
  ✓ the proposer of the Motion;
  ✓ the opposer of the Motion;
  ✓ the seconder of the Motion;
  ✓ the seconder of the opposition;
  ✓ any speakers from the floor in the order in which they are called by the Chair;
  ✓ the proposer of the Motion to sum up the case for;
  ✓ the opposer of the Motion to sum up the case against.
- A vote will then be taken at the end of the debate. In a case of a tie, the Chair has a casting vote.

Theme 6: What's Your Opinion?

CHOOSING A SUBJECT

You need to find a subject about which members of the class are divided in their opinions. Once you have found a subject, you make it into a proposition for debate by making a statement with which some will agree and some will disagree. For example:

Subject: *Hunting of foxes.*
Proposition: *Hunting of foxes should be banned.*

☆ RESEARCH

An uninformed debate is worse than useless - it can be dangerous. Everyone who might take part - **and that means everyone** - needs to check on facts that might be useful. So you need to allow time for this. No-one wants to be caught out when the debate starts.

CONTRIBUTORS

Of course, anyone has a right to contribute to the debate, but the following people must be identified beforehand:
- ✔ Chair
- ✔ Proposer and seconder
- ✔ Opposer and seconder.

THE DEBATE

Good luck!
- Try to produce facts as evidence for opinion; avoid mere statement of opinion on its own.
- Once the vote has been taken, it would be interesting to find out how many people changed their opinions as a result of the debate.

REMEMBER: Only people with closed minds never change their opinions.

7.1 Perceptions.

This unit examines how different people perceive things in different ways. You will be thinking about the way literature can help us see the world in fresh and unusual ways.

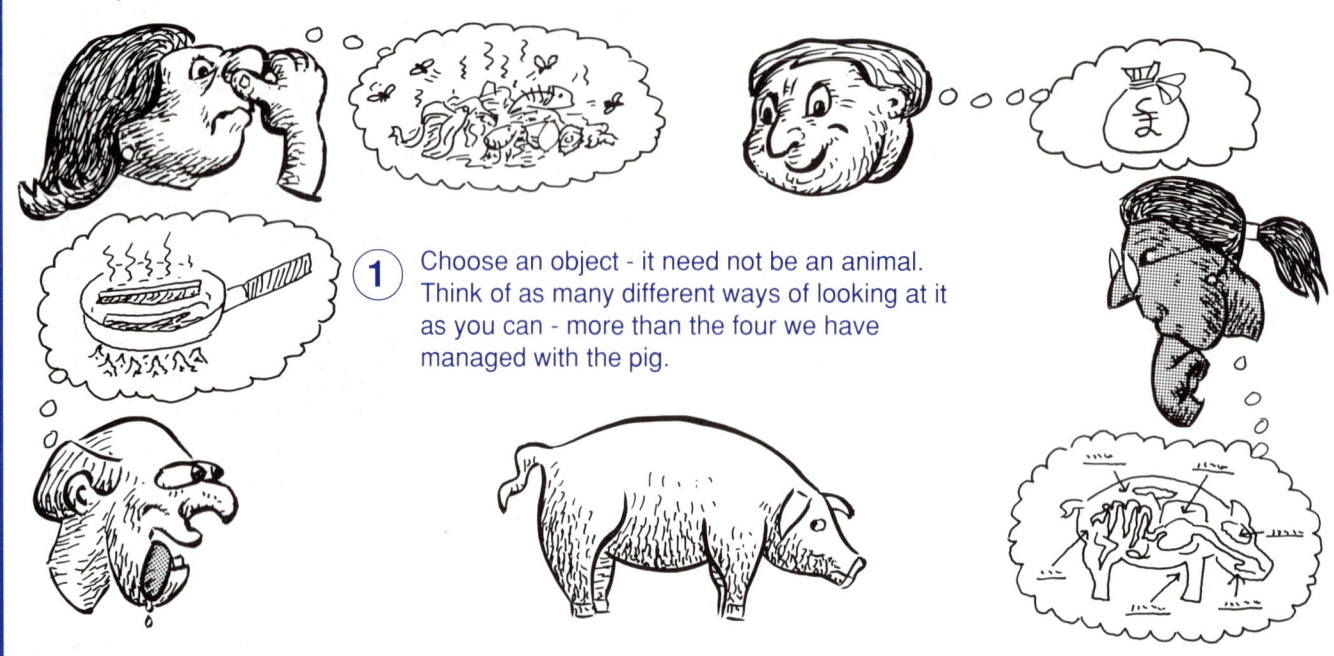

1 Choose an object - it need not be an animal. Think of as many different ways of looking at it as you can - more than the four we have managed with the pig.

The Swiss artist, Erhard Jacoby, has taken this idea further. His painting (A) illustrates the fact that each of us perceives the world in a slightly different way from the others. A camera from the same position would have recorded faithfully everything in front of the lens. The human eye sees everything in front of it much like a camera but the brain selects certain details.

A

Theme 7: Perceptions

2. Find a picture which shows a variety of activities going on, e.g. a busy street scene.
   ☆
   - Ask different people, including adults, to look at the picture for about five seconds and then recall as much detail as they can.
   - Do different people notice different things?
   - Is there any sort of pattern to the sorts of things people notice?

3. In **A**, the actual position of the three people changes slightly what they see, but there are also some subtle differences in terms of what they notice. How many of these can you find?

4. Imagine that immediately after the scene shown, there is a crash at the intersection. The three simple diagrams, **B, C** and **D,** show that each of the three different witnesses imagine that the accident has happened in slightly different ways.
   - Write a statement to go with each of the diagrams using the first person. E.g. *"I was standing on the pavement waiting to cross the road when ..."*

5. If the police wanted to establish which version was accurate how would they go about doing so?
   - In groups of four roleplay the necessary interviews and try to come to a conclusion.

6. Think of an area in the school with which most people in the class are familiar. A front entrance hall or a display area would do.
   - Write down as many details as possible about the area - colour of walls, doors, posters, etc.
   - In groups of five or six, pool your knowledge to get a detailed description of your area.
   - Which group's description is the most accurate?
   - How many inaccuracies does each group's description contain?

7. Now take the same area and write three paragraphs describing the way it might be seen by:
   - a visitor coming into the school for the first time
   - a pupil who has been kept behind in the area for misbehaving
   - a cleaner.

7.2 Seeing Yourself.

Most people do not like the sound of their own voices on a tape recorder and are often critical of themselves: *"I did not know I sounded so squeaky - deep - high-pitched - rough - nasal ..."*
Other people listening to the same recording often do not notice the same things. You might like to try and see. Do they hear the same sounds? Strictly speaking, yes, but in another way they are "hearing" different sounds just as people "see" differently. When you look in the mirror what do you "see"? It is hard to be honest about ourselves even in terms of physical appearance; people tend to be either insecure about themselves or (probably less often) conceited.
The following extract is from the novel *A Kind of Loving* by Stan Barstow. Do we learn anything about the personality of the character from what is written here? Can you guess when it was written?

The first thing I do when I go upstairs is take a look at myself in the dressing-table mirror. It's one of those with three glasses in and if you get the knack of adjusting them you can see what you look like from the side as well as straight on. It seems to me I'm spending altogether too much time these days either looking in mirrors at home or catching sight of myself in mirrors outside. I never knew there were so many mirrors; the world's full of them, or shop windows with the blinds down, which amount to the same thing as far as what I'm talking about's concerned. When I'm washing my hands at the office I can see another pair of hands just like mine doing the same. If I go to the pictures ten to one I'll climb the stairs and come face to face with my twin brother coming up from the other side. (Only he's not strictly my twin because he's the opposite hand to me.) And I've only to look out of a bus at night to see this same opposite-handed me looking in from outside. It's not that I'm conceited - at least, not most of the time - and when I see myself in a window or something I don't think what a swell-looking geezer, but try to look at myself as though I'm somebody else and wonder what I think of me. And it's actually that I'm NOT a swell-looking geezer. At least, not most of the time. I never used to be like this. I can remember when I didn't give a monkey's what I looked like or what anybody thought of me. But now it's different; because now, you see, I'm conscious of women. Very conscious of them in fact.

When I'm looking in my mirror at home like I am now, I don't think I'm so bad. Whichever way you look, and whoever's doing the looking, you couldn't call me ugly. Not HANDSOME, maybe, but not ugly. My face is sort of square and what an author might call open, and it's a good colour. (Thank God I'm not one of these blokes who's plagued to death with boils and spots and blains and whatnot.) The scar over my left eye where I argued with the railing doesn't help, though I wonder sometimes if it doesn't make me look a bit tougher. I don't know.

And there's always my hair. No two ways about that, I've got a head of hair any man would be proud of, thick and dark with a natural wave that only needs a touch of the fingers after it's combed and glossy without a lot of cream. No doubt about my hair. And I have it cut every fortnight and never miss. Or only now and again. I could do with a couple more inches on my height. I've always had a yen for just two more inches. But still I'm not a little runt because I've got a good build - a nice deep chest that I'm not scared of showing off in swimming trunks, and square broad shoulders. And my clothes. Now there's no denying I know how to dress. I don't pay the earth for my suits but I know where they give you the right cut and I always keep my pants pressed and my shoes clean. And if my shirt's just the least bit grubby at the collar, into the wash it goes. Ask the Old Lady. She says it's like washing for an army keeping up to me alone.

So there I am - Victor Arthur Brown, twenty years old, one of the lads, and not very sure of himself under the cocky talk and dirty jokes and wisecracks. Take me or leave me, I'm all I've got.

Theme 7: Perceptions

① Draw a spider graph with Victor Arthur Brown at the centre, and words or statements about his personality all around him.

② Try writing two contrasting descriptions which both begin: "When I look in the mirror ..." They should both be about the same person - yourself if you like. In the first one the person is feeling very depressed. In the second one, that same person is feeling very conceited.

③ Is there anything about the style and content of the passage and the attitude of the character which indicates when it was written?

THOUGHT ASSOCIATIONS

There is a story about a group of philosophers from ancient times who were very concerned that they should not be misunderstood. But they knew that whenever they uttered any word at all, people would form slightly different images in their minds. For example, if one of them used the word "knife", listeners might imagine a carving knife, a table knife, a sheath knife, and so on. This worried these pedantic philosophers no end, until they hit upon a solution to their problem.

They decided to carry around with them a large sack each, full of everything that they might wish to talk about. Then, each time any one of them spoke, he scrabbled in his sack and produced the object about which he was speaking. So they all knew that they were thinking about exactly the same thing. Unfortunately it also constrained them in their travels because their sacks became rather large and heavy ... Well, that's the story, anyway. But the point it is intended to illustrate is important. Even if a listener thinks s/he understands a speaker perfectly, in all sorts of ways, obvious and more subtle, their understandings are different.

④ Take each of the words below in turn and without giving it any thought, write down immediately a few notes telling what images the word conjures up in your mind. Do this quickly with a time limit of five minutes for the complete list. Then compare your notes with your neighbour's and see how you think along similar or different lines, given the same stimulus.

- hotel
- dog
- river
- game
- boat

Do your neighbour's reactions tell you anything about her or him? Could your notes on any of these words be extended and developed into a short poem?

7.3 The Perception Transfer.

This extract is the start of a book set in the future; but the book is still unfinished. The threat of global war has diminished, but another problem has taken its place: the destabilising effects of terrorism, now used by many governments as a routine part of their foreign policies.

Dr. Choudhuri carefully lifted the Perception-Transfer and fitted it over her head. It left only her mouth, nose and eyes visible. She felt a shiver of panic and quickly removed it.

"Can we just go over it once more?" she asked Professor Barnes. "I'll be left alone with the prisoner. The guards will be immediately available if needed. I sit opposite him across the table, put on the P-T and concentrate entirely on him. Is that really all there is to it?"

"That's all," said the Professor. "Then it's just a matter of seeing how it works. I'll end the session after fifteen minutes as agreed. Good luck." He rose and left the doctor alone in the small bare room, furnished only with a table and two chairs; there were no windows.

Dr. Choudhuri knew the risks. The prisoner had been convicted of terrorism - in fact he had planted a bomb which had killed three people and injured many more. That had been three years ago in 2015. It had to be assumed that he had been involved in many other plots prior to that. And if he did decide to attack, there was no way of knowing how quickly - or indeed whether - someone in the Perception-Transfer phase would be able to react. The safety button might prove to give a false sense of security. But that was not her chief fear. The P-T had not been tested except in controlled laboratory conditions. No-one was quite certain how it might work out in field trials. There were always risks involved - both psychological and physical. But if it worked, then it would be a much needed breakthrough in terrorist control. That would be particularly welcome now all the major powers were heavily involved in terrorism; it had become an accepted weapon of foreign policy. If the P-T really enabled captors to visualise the world through their captives' eyes regardless of what they were thinking about at the time, then the routine torture, which had become so commonplace worldwide, would be eliminated; it would, quite simply, be unnecessary. But what exactly did it mean, "to visualise the world through their captives' eyes"? No-one really knew. And what effect might it have on either of them? Again, no-one knew.

Her thoughts were interrupted as the prisoner was led in, taken round to the other side of the table, and told to sit down. He did so without a trace of emotion. He didn't even look at Dr. Choudhuri. At a sign from her, the guards left the room and closed the door. Dr. Choudhuri placed the P-T over her head and concentrated her eyes and all her attention on the prisoner. The ordeal had begun.

Gradually the figure opposite began to blur and become hazy as if viewed through a dense fog. For some moments that was all. And then, quite effortlessly, Dr. Choudhuri saw that she was out in the open, in a city street somewhere and she was moving along it. Her fears slipped away as she became totally involved in the new world.

She could tell she was in a street, but by no means was everything clear. The street itself appeared generally vague - mostly rather foggy and indistinct, though some parts of it were clearly and sharply focused. For example, there was a Police Station a little way ahead, brightly lit and with every detail clearly defined.

But it was the people who startled her. There were many about, all apparently hurrying in different directions, but without exception they were grey shapes, unclear and with no visible features. Where a face should be was no more than a whitish blur.

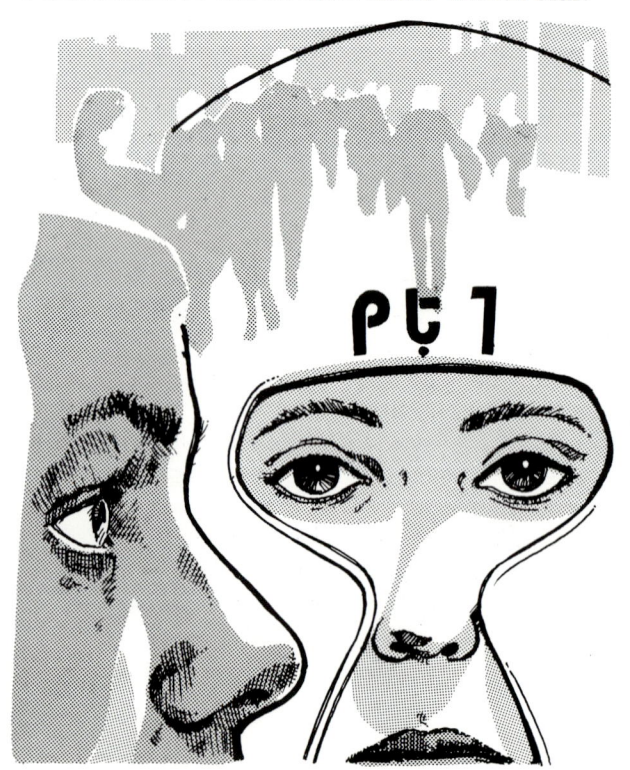

Theme 7: Perceptions

The traffic, too, was formless. It existed, but that was about all. Dr. Choudhuri could not even distinguish the individual transits from the communal carriers. They were all just dark shapes, speeding past. Or, rather, most of them were. One exception was coming towards her, and she could see plainly it was an army riot control unit - the sort that had come into regular service around the turn of the century when terrorism had become the main threat to world survival. The doctor found that she was unable to take her eyes and total attention away from the vehicle until it had passed her and disappeared round the corner. Only then could she look round again.

She was now standing by the Police Station she had noticed earlier. The entrance was immediately to her right. She was able to note every detail of it, the steps, the marks on the stones, even the precise symbols on the computer-controlled entry portal. Then her attention was again involuntarily attracted to a grating on the pavement just by the doorway, a grating on which she could see scratches in the rusty metal. It appeared to have been moved recently.

For some reason she could not explain, she felt it necessary to move away quickly, and on she went up the road. A dog approached her, wagging its tail. It was a King Charles spaniel, she noticed, with distinctive brown markings. Without thinking she bent down to stroke it, but it walked straight past, ignoring her. With her attention thus distracted, she appeared to bump into a woman pushing a baby portabed, though the woman didn't seem to notice. Then something strange happened. The woman's face had been a blur like all the others, and her body a grey, ill-defined shape. But momentarily Dr. Choudhuri saw a real face - an attractive face of a woman in her early twenties, both friendly and serene. She was wearing a close-fitting, bright red Actionclad which showed off her youthful figure to advantage. For just a moment, the doctor felt she was about to make human contact and then, for no apparent reason, the image faded; the woman's face became an expressionless blur like everyone else's, and her body a shapeless, grey smudge.

At that moment she felt, rather than heard, the explosion. But she had no chance to react because, almost simultaneously, the entire scene vanished. Beside her was standing Professor Barnes; he had just removed the P-T and was holding it in his hands. She had been warned about this. The wearer was unable to end the experience because of the total involvement it demanded; this had to be done by another person, at least until a more efficient system had been developed.

Doctor Choudhuri fought to control her emotions and to stem the tears which threatened. For a few moments she looked at the prisoner and felt very close to him. But he did not respond. His eyes were dead and cold as if she - and everyone else - just didn't exist for him.

1 ☆ Following her experience Dr. Choudhuri was required to make a report interpreting what she had seen. All she had been able to do in the passage was to see things through the terrorist's eyes. Now she had to reach a stage further into his mind and try to answer this question.
- Why did he see things in that way?
  ✓ Write her report explaining what she saw.
  ✓ Set it out in two columns.

2 In the story the Perception-Transfer has been used in a serious situation. But that needn't always be so. If you were to get hold of a P-T you could have a lot of fun visualising the world as someone else might see it. Choose someone to use it on and write up what happened.

Now try . . . . . .

3 ☆ This extract is from a book set in the future. But the rest of the book has not been written and maybe never will be. Continue the idea and develop it into a proper story. If you do this, you will need plenty of time to develop the idea.

7.4 Metaphor.

Sometimes a poet describes a subject by comparing it with something that is quite different except in certain respects. The two ideas - the subject and whatever the poet is using to help describe the subject - exist together in the poem. It can be quite difficult to disentangle which is which. The following poems illustrate the point.

The fog comes
on little cat feet.
It sits looking
over harbour and city
on silent haunches
and then moves on.

Carl Sandburg

Subtle as an illusionist
The deft hands of the morning mist
Play tricks upon my sight:
Haystacks dissolve and hedges lift
Out of unseen fields and drift
Between the veils of white.

On the horizon, heads of trees
Swim with the mist about their knees
And the farm-dogs bark,
I turn to watch how on the calm
Of that white sea, the red-roofed farm
Floats like a Noah's Ark.

Douglas Gibson

Curling softly,
The fog gently winds itself around my legs.
It rubs its face along the walls
and slides along the street,
Drifting,
Blurring the lighted windows
As it purrs to be let in.
Rejected from the warmth,
It hisses around the gas lamps
and sneaks off towards the horizon.

Jitendra Patel

1 Choose one of the poems on this page.
- Draw 2 columns.
- At the top of the first one, write what is the real **subject** of the poem.
- At the top of the second one write what **image** the poet uses to help to describe the subject.
- Now note down what the poem says about each heading.

2 You should have now disentangled the 2 ideas in the poem.
- ✔ The **subject** is the **literal meaning**.
- ✔ The **comparison** in column 2, is the poet's chosen **metaphor**.
- Does the metaphor help you to see the subject in a new light?

Theme 7: Perceptions

Here is another poem, in which the poet has emphasised his meaning with a pun in the title.

A Local Train of Thought

Alone, in silence, at a certain time of night,
Listening, and looking up from what I'm trying to write,
I hear a local train along the Valley. And "There
Goes the one-fifty," think I to myself; aware
That somehow its habitual travelling comforts me,
Making my world seem safer, homelier, sure to be
The same tomorrow; and the same, one hopes, next year.
"There's peacetime in that train." One hears it disappear
With needless warning whistle and rail-resounding wheels.
"That train's quite like an old familiar friend," one feels.

Siegfried Sassoon

3 If the poet had made notes before writing the poem he could well have made them under the heading *"What the train means to me"*. Write the notes he might have made.

4 Now try a similar process for yourself.
- ✔ Choose a subject which is quite ordinary but which means more to you because of its associations for you.
- ✔ Make notes about these associations.
- ✔ Organise the notes so that they form a piece of verse. Decide whether you want to write in free verse or make your poem rhyme.

Because people perceive reality in different ways, we can never be certain about anything. Nor can we be sure that we are being understood adequately when we are speaking to anyone. This unit has given you plenty of examples. This last activity is to do with the differing perceptions of young people and older people. It starts with role play and then goes on to the writing of a script.

Now try . . . . . .

5 In pairs you need to decide together about the following.
- ✓ Two people - one older and one your age.
- ✓ A subject about which they have very different perceptions because of their different generations.
- Role play a discussion between them, in which each is trying to understand why the other thinks as s/he does.
- Develop your discussion into a play script for radio in which the different perceptions of the two people are explored.

8.1 It's Your Life!

An autobiography is his/her account of his/her own life story. In this unit you will be looking at various aspects of autobiography which will lead eventually to a major piece of autobiographical writing.

If you look back on your life so far you will have sad and happy memories. Some things will be very memorable, others you will only recollect in a hazy fashion. Some memories may be very private and personal so it will be up to you to decide what details you will include in the autobiography which will be read by other people. You may decide that you do not want to write about yourself at all but would prefer to invent a character on whom the autobiography is based. You could make that decision later.

1 ☆ Make some notes on your life so far. You will find that you can remember a great deal more than you think once you start to jot down memories. Write as many notes as you can on each of these questions. Try to draw on your memories of when you were under ten years of age.
- What is your earliest memory?
- What was your favourite toy when you were young?
- Can you remember your first day at school?
- Can you remember any accidents you had?
- Can you remember any fight or argument you had?
- What Christmas or Feast Day stands out most in your memory?
- Do you have any particularly happy memory?
- Do you have any particularly sad memory?
- How many houses or areas have you lived in so far in your life?
- Did you have a "favourite place" when you were young?

2 Jot down any other random memories.
- ✔ details of friends
- ✔ shops you liked to go to
- ✔ places you went to play
- ✔ relatives who came to visit
- ✔ teachers you had
- ✔ a time when you got lost.

3 Now represent your life in the form of a drawing or diagram as if it is a journey with small drawings representing different happenings as in A.

4 Now that you have assembled as many details as you can you should talk to parents or relatives who may be able to supply details about your early life which you do not know. You may be able to find photographs which jog your memory.

Theme 8: It's Your Life!

FACT OR FICTION?

Charles Dickens said that autobiography is a matter of weaving together truth and fiction. What he meant was that although the basic facts and memories may be correct, the writer will often tend to elaborate on the details in order to capture the appropriate mood.

Version A

Looking back, as I was saying, into the blank of my infancy, the first objects I can remember as standing out by themselves from a confusion of things, are my mother and Peggotty. What else do I remember? Let me see. There comes out of the cloud our house - not new to me, but quite familiar in its earliest remembrance. On the ground-floor is Peggotty's kitchen, opening into a back yard; with a pigeon-house on a pole, in the centre, without any pigeons in it; a great dog-kennel in a corner, without any dog; and a quantity of fowls that look terribly tall to me, walking about in a menacing and ferocious manner. There is one cock who gets upon a post to crow, and seems to take particular notice of me as I look at him through the kitchen window, who makes me shiver he is so fierce. Of the geese outside the side-gate who come waddling after me with their long necks stretched out when I go that way, I dream at night: as a man environed by wild beasts might dream of lions.

Version B

I can remember Peggotty's kitchen opening into the back yard with a pigeon-house and dog-kennel. I can also remember in that yard a number of fowls, a cock and geese.

5 Imagine that you are the author of version A which has been returned to you by your editor with a suggested shorter version B which will save space. Write your reply justifying the longer version.

Now try . . . . . .

6 Write a short paragraph of your own which begins "When I look back into the earliest days of my childhood the first objects I can remember…"

7 You have tried to recall details of your early childhood. Can you remember events which you associate with particularly strong emotions?
Can you remember times
✔ when you were frightened?
✔ when you were lost?
✔ when you had a nightmare?
✔ when you did not understand what was going on in the adult world?
✔ when you felt left out by family or friends?

61

8.2 Remembering People.

1. Choose an adult who made a fairly strong impression on you when you were young - it could be a teacher, a neighbour or even someone you never actually spoke to but remember well.
- Write three sentences describing that character and then read the following description by various authors which evoke vividly some colourful people.

I vaguely remember my first teacher - a bosomy, red-haired lady with protruding teeth and a jolly face. She frightened me. Her voice was so shockingly loud and clear and brisk, after the playful gentleness of my mother's, and she had no trace of Geordie accent. She spoke in such a refined voice that for several days, until I got used to it, I couldn't understand what she was saying.

James Kirkup

Although she was my aunt, I never thought of her as anything but the wife of my uncle, partly because he was so big and trumpeting and redhairy and used to fill every inch of the hot little house like an old buffalo squeezed into an airing cupboard, and partly because she was so small and silk and quick and made no noise at all as she whisked about on padded paws, dusting the china dogs, feeding the buffalo, setting the mousetraps that never caught her; and once she sleaked out of the room, to squeak in a nook or nibble in the hayloft, you forgot she had ever been there.

Dylan Thomas

Mr Squeers's appearance was not prepossessing. He had but one eye and the popular prejudice runs in favour of two. The eye he had was unquestionably useful, but decidedly not ornamental; being of a greenish grey, and in shape resembling the fan-light of a street door. The blank side of his face was much wrinkled and puckered up, which gave him a very sinister appearance, especially when he smiled, at which times his expression bordered on the villainous. His hair was very flat and shiny, save at the ends, where it was brushed stiffly up from a low protruding forehead, which assorted well with his harsh voice and coarse manner. He was about two or three and fifty and a trifle below the middle size; he wore a white neckerchief with long ends, and a suit of scholastic black; but his coat sleeves being a great deal too long, and his trousers a great deal too short, he appeared ill at ease in his clothes, and as if he were in a perpetual state of astonishment at finding himself so respectable.

Charles Dickens

She was a bunched and punitive little body and the school had christened her Crabby; she had a sour yellow look, lank hair coiled in earphones, and the skin and voice of a turkey. We were all afraid of the gobbling Miss B.; she spied, she pried, she crouched, she crept, she pounced - she was a terror.

Laurie Lee

62

Theme 8: It's Your Life!

There was also the piano teacher who used to come down once a week on the train from Dublin. I remember little about him except for his ineffectiveness as a teacher and the reason for his going. My mother would come into the drawing-room towards the end of each lesson and sigh restlessly from her chair, fretted by my lack of progress. He was a nervous man who became almost insane in her presence. His hands would shake, and he would begin to tear distractedly at the dark stains of hardened food that decorated the front of his jacket as he watched me play. The drawing-room smelt of applewood and turf, and, in the autumn, the bitter end-of-the-year smell of chrysanthemums which stood in pots massed in one of the deep bay windows, shades of yellow, gold, bronze and white, like a second fir in the room. The black ebony case of the Steinway grand reflected the flowers. The music teacher was ridiculously out of place.

Jennifer Johnston

He used to sit all day, looking out from behind the dirty little window of his dirty little shop in Main Street; a man with a smooth oval pate and bleared, melancholy-looking, unblinking eyes; a hanging lip with a fag dangling from it, and hanging unshaven chins. It was a face you'd remember; swollen, ponderous, crimson, with a frame of jet-black hair plastered down on either side with bear's grease; and though the hair grew grey and the face turned yellow it seemed to make no difference: because he never changed position you did not notice the changes that came over him from within, and saw him at the end as you had seen him at first, planted there like an oak or a rock. He scarcely stirred even when someone pushed in the old glazed door and stumbled down the steps from the street. The effort seemed to be too much for him; the bleary bloodshot eyes travelled slowly to some shelf, the arm reached lifelessly out; the coins dropped in the till. Then he shrugged himself and gazed out into the street again. Sometimes he spoke, and it always gave you a shock, for it was as if the statue of O'Connell had descended from its pedestal and inquired in a melancholy bass voice and with old-fashioned politeness for some member of your family. It was a thing held greatly in his favour that he never forgot an old neighbour.

Frank O'Connor

2 Notice the different stylistic techniques the different authors use. For practice complete the following in your own words - use a phrase not just a single word.
- His face was full and fat...
- He had a thick beard like...
- Her voice was so soft...
- We were afraid of the ferocious Mr. Barton...
- He bellowed, he roared, he...
- His old, torn jacket was studded with...
- He used to fill every inch of the house like...

3 Write two or three more sentences to continue each of the descriptions then swap what you have written with a partner and try to work out which passage the descriptions accompany.

4 Using the notes you made earlier, write a paragraph of vivid description of your own based on someone you remember from your past or on a character you invent.

8.3 Structure and Style.

Many autobiographies are written in chronological order - that is they follow the events as they happened in a person's life. It often makes a more interesting opening if you begin with a particular incident and then go back to cover details which came earlier.

So instead of *"I was born in Dryburn hospital on 3rd June 1981 at 3 minutes past midnight...."*, you could begin *"All the trouble began when my grandfather died and my grandmother came to visit us..."*. Or *"If it hadn't been for the lego train set I received that Christmas I probably would at this moment in time be living in New York in America..."*

1 WHEN I WAS THREE I WAS SAVED FROM A FIRE.	2 I WAS IN HOSPITAL FOR FOUR WEEKS.	3 TEN YEARS LATER I WAS BACK THERE...	4 AND ENDED UP LIMPING AROUND ON CRUTCHES.
1 AS I SIT HERE WITH MY LEG IN PLASTER...	2 I THINK BACK TO THE ACCIDENT.	3 THE ONLY OTHER TIME I WAS IN HOSPITAL...	4 WAS AFTER THE AWFUL FIRE.

The following passage is the opening paragraph of Christopher Nolan's autobiography, *Under The Eye of the Clock*. He received brain damage at birth which left his body paralysed. He writes by typing with a unicorn stick attached to his head. He wrote his autobiography at the age of 18. He begins his autobiography with an event which happened when he was older, a journey home with his mother after receiving a literary prize in London.

> Can you credit all of the fuss that was made of a cripple, mused Joseph Meehan as he settled his back against the seat for the flight home to Dublin. Now he had gained enough confidence to ask Nora to order a cup of coffee for him. Heretofore he had always declined any offer of refreshments, fearful always of creating a scene if fluid swallowed awkwardly went against his breath. "Tea or coffee?" enquired the Aer Lingus hostess. "Coffee, two coffees please," said Nora. It came as a surprise to Nora when Joseph indicated in his silent code that he was bold enough now to attempt the arduous feat for him of swallowing down something in public. As the mother sensed his new-found bravery, she determined to pour small slurps of the coffee into his nervous mouth.
> Determinedly he smuggled the beverage past his decidedly stubborn tongue and let it slip down into his stomach. Snuggling his head then against the seat he slyly slipped away from Nora and scrambled silk blessings from cotton-wool casts.

NOTICE
✓ that the author writes about himself in the third person
✓ that the autobiography is not written chronologically
✓ that it starts with the description of drinking a cup of coffee in public - a symbol of his "new-found bravery", rather than "I was born on..."
✓ the unusual way the author chooses to describe the act of going to sleep in the last two lines.

Theme 8: It's Your Life!

In the following extract from Arthur Miller's autobiography *Timebends* notice the way the author concentrates on the appearance of things as they appear to a young child.

> The view from the floor is of a pair of pointy black calf-height shoes, one of them twitching restlessly, and just above them the plum-colored skirt rising from the ankles to the blouse, and higher still the young round face and her ever-changing tones of voice as she gossips into the wall telephone with one of her two sisters, something she would go on doing the rest of her life until one by one they peeled off the wire and vanished into the sky. Now she looks down at me looking up at her from the foyer floor, bends over and tries to move me clear of her foot. But I must lie on her shoe, and from far up above through skirt and darkness I hear her laughing pleasantly at my persistence.

NOTICE
- ✔ that the present tense is used
- ✔ the original beginning as opposed to *"I was born in New York in..."*
- ✔ the paragraph is written literally from the point of view of a young child on the floor

Here are two more examples of openings to get you thinking:

I can remember feeling very angry with my father when I first discovered that cats eyes in the road are not really made by killing cats, and that the noise from the central heating in our house was not really a ghost. I learned that you cannot always trust adults, even the ones who are very close to you. Later in life, the truth of that realisation was confirmed in a cruel and unexpected way ...

"Daddy, I'm thirsty."
"Daddy, I want a drink of water."
"DAD!"
"I'll be up in a minute."
Each night I struggled to find some excuse to bring my father back into the bedroom. I was desperate for the lights to come on to bring some brief comfort from the terrors induced by the "pooky" stories told by my sister; these were tales of ghosts and wolves and terrifying ghouls which would tear your heart out. She was seven. I was five ...

① Write four possible openings to your own autobiography. Here are some suggestions:
a conventional opening "I was born on..."
- ✔ an opening which starts with something which happened recently in your life
- ✔ an opening which starts with conversation
- ✔ an opening which starts with the present tense
- ✔ an opening which starts with some seemingly trivial event
- ✔ an opening which starts from the viewpoint of a young child.

8.4 Other People's Lives.

Autobiographies which are well written do not just tell us about the facts of a person's life but they convey something about how it felt to be young and what it felt like to live at a particular time and place.

James Kirkup writes about life on Tyneside in the 1950s:

> I wore a new woollen guernsey - "gansey" is the name given to it on Tyneside - which buttoned on the shoulder with three mother-of-pearl buttons. My mother had knitted it for me. It reminded me of her, and as I sat in that hideous classroom I felt the contrast between the love of home and the indifference of school so strongly that I had great difficulty in restraining my tears. No one had told me about the lavatory, and I remember looking down at the floor and being astonished to see it all wet under my feet; a little boy sitting next to me jumped up and shouted: "Please, miss, 'e's wet the floor!"

Alex Haley, in his novel *Roots* which describes the history of his ancestors from their origins in Africa to life in America, remembers his early life.

> Even before I could talk, Grandma would say years later, he would carry me in his arms down to the lumber company, where he built a crib to put me in while he took care of business. After I had learned to walk, we would go together downtown, me taking three steps to each of his, my small fist tightly grasped about his extended left forefinger. Looming over me like a black, tall strong tree, Grandpa would stop and chat with people we met along the way. Grandpa taught me to look anyone right in their eyes, to speak to them clearly and politely. Sometimes people exclaimed how well raised I was and how fine I was growing up. "Well, I guess he'll do," Grandpa would respond.

1. Try to write details of a particular item of clothing you wore as a child, a visit you made to the country or seaside or town, a time when you made up stories to impress your friends.

2. A biography is an account of someone's life written by another person. Choose one of these passages and rewrite it as if it is from their biography. You will need to write in the third person but you will find that there are other changes you will need to make.

Theme 8: It's Your Life!

LETTERS

Letters can be a valuable way of finding out about someone's life. Because the intended audience for the letter knows the context it is necessary for other readers to guess what has been going on. What follows is a fictitious letter from a prisoner.

> Dear Eve,
>
> At last I am able to write to you after the extraordinary events of the last two weeks. You'll have read about the riots in the papers but don't believe everything you read. As far as I know (and as a relative newcomer here I certainly don't know everything) there was no advance planning. The rioting just happened as a spontaneous response to the terrible conditions here.
>
> I am still in a cell with two other prisoners. It is cramped with little room other than for our bunks and a bucket in the corner. It's getting a little better now in that my two "friends" are past the stage of threatening me. Having established that I am not likely to challenge them in any way and that basically I am not a "hard man" they are leaving me alone. They are in for armed robbery and assault and were amused when I claimed I was innocent of any crime.
>
> How are the plans for the appeal going? I am sorry that you are left with so much to do but Mr. Hartop should take care of most of the paper work. I had a long talk with him three weeks ago and he seems to be fairly hopeful. He is thinking of contacting the media for some publicity and help. My defence at the trial would have been better if they had more expert evidence on the precise time of death. He is looking in to that.
>
> Back to the riot. It is funny to think how one single act can set off such a chain of events. One of the prisoners (a "lifer" I've learned to call him) simply refused to pick up his tray and that started it. I didn't join them on the roof at any stage and am hoping that I won't be accused of taking part. It could prolong my sentence.
>
> I look forward to your letters. You are the only one I really have now who I feel I can trust.
>
> Love,
>
> Simon.

3 In pairs work out what might have happened in the past which explains the content of the letter.

4 Write the reply which Eve sent. In your letter you should try to convey as much as you can about what life is like in society at the time of writing.

5 Imagine the two letters were found 100 years later and were reprinted in a history book. Write a brief paragraph to go with them indicating what they show about life in the 1990s.

Now try . . . . . .

6 ☆ Write your own autobiography based on the notes you have made so far. Make decisions about
- first or third person
- direct speech
- order of events

You do not have to write about very personal affairs to make the life story interesting - it is up to you what you include. Do not forget to write a draft and rework your autobiography.

7 Write an autobiography which is completely invented. It will be even more important to plan and draft your written work here.

8 Compose a series of letters written by someone in a particular situation to a friend or relative, which convey something of the life and times of that person.

9.1 Writing for Children.

In this unit you will think about what makes a good children's story and write some of your own. You will give particular attention to levels of language difficulty.

The following extracts were taken from stories written for young children of different ages.

A

Yok-Yok is playing with a frog. They are on a water-lily. The water-lily is in the middle of a pond. The pond is blue. Yok-yok sees a fly. He tells the frog. The frog eats the fly. Yok-yok laughs.

B

Meg wouldn't give in. The little terrier was equally determined.
"I dug most of the hole so I should own it."
"Yes, but I found the opening in the first place and told you about it."
Nel, the other collie, made a second rather feeble attempt at making peace. "Couldn't we take it in turns?" she asked.

C

Jack and Helen went ahead to find a cave where they could all spend the night. It was starting to get dark and the prospect of sleeping outside again did not appeal to any of them. Although hungry and tired, they were determined to keep going. Since early morning not one of them had mentioned the screams they had heard during the night.

1. What age group is each story suitable for in your opinion?

2. ★ Which of these stories might be easiest/most difficult for a child who is learning to read? You will need to consider which extract uses the simplest/most complex language, and comment on the vocabulary and sentence structure.

3. From the extracts given what do you think might appeal to children about each of these stories?

4. Make a list of the stories you enjoyed most when you were young and the age you were when you read them.

5. What makes a good children's story? List as many ideas as you can and compare these with a partner.

Theme 9: Writing for Children

Children's stories can make a serious point as well as entertain. The following scenes come from *Not Now, Bernard* by David McKee.
Bernard keeps getting ignored by his parents. Every time he approaches them they say, "Not now, Bernard." This is the way the story ends.

The monster ate Bernard up, every bit.

Then the monster went indoors and was dragged upstairs by Bernard's mother and put to bed.

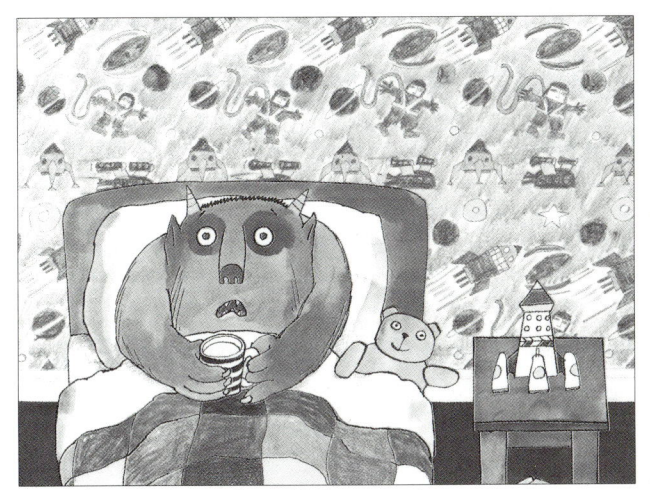

"But I'm a monster," said the monster.

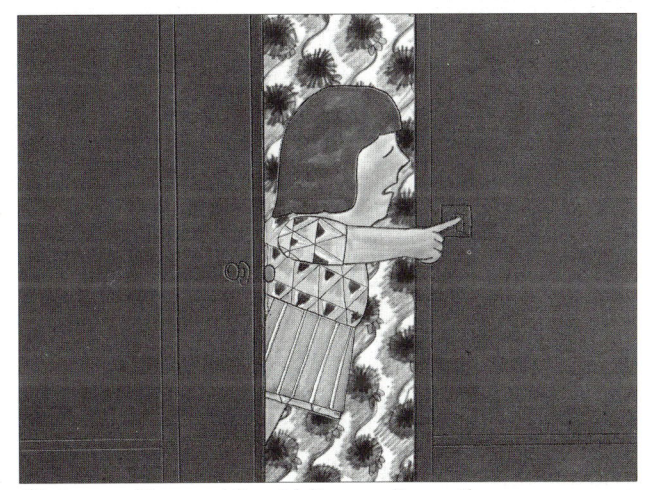

"Not now, Bernard," said Bernard's mother.

6 Write two versions of text to go with the story which can be read by children themselves. One is for 6 year olds who are just beginning to read, the other for 8 year olds who can read quite fluently.

7 Does your version of the story make a serious point?

8 Only part of the story is printed here. Can you suggest any other scenes which would have been appropriate?

Now try . . . . . .

9 Imagine that you are preparing a catalogue of children's books. Each entry will require details of language, story, pictures, presentation, format, size, print, likely appeal, value for money. Choose some children's books and write entries for the catalogue.

9.2 The Story Teller.

Have you ever had to look after young children when they have been restless and difficult? Could you tell a story which would keep young children entertained? In the following story by Saki, the aunt of three young children is finding it difficult to keep them amused when a stranger intervenes.

It was a hot afternoon, and the railway carriage was correspondingly sultry, and the next stop was at Templecombe, nearly an hour ahead. The occupants of the carriage were a small girl, and a smaller girl, and a small boy. An aunt belonging to the children occupied one corner seat, and the further corner seat on the opposite side was occupied by a bachelor who was a stranger to their party, but the small girls and the boy emphatically occupied the compartment. Both the aunt and the children were conversational in a limited, persistent way, reminding one of the attentions of a housefly that refused to be discouraged. Most of the aunt's remarks seemed to begin with "Don't," and nearly all of the children's remarks began with "Why?" The bachelor said nothing out loud.

"Don't, Cyril, don't," exclaimed the aunt, as the small boy began smacking the cushions of the seat, producing a cloud of dust at each blow.

"Come and look out of the window," she added.

The child moved reluctantly to the window. "Why are those sheep being driven out of that field?" he asked.

"I expect they are being driven to another field where there is more grass," the aunt said weakly.

"But there is lots of grass in that field," protested the boy; "there's nothing else but grass there. Aunt, there's lots of grass in that field."

"Perhaps the grass in the other field is better," suggested the aunt, fatuously.

"Why is it better?" came the swift, inevitable question.

"Oh, look at those cows!" exclaimed the aunt. Nearly every field along the line had contained cows or bullocks, but she spoke as though she were drawing attention to a rarity.

"Why is the grass in the other field better?" Cyril persisted.

The frown on the bachelor's face was deepening to a scowl. He was a hard unsympathetic man, the aunt decided in her mind. She was utterly unable to come to any decision about the grass in the other field.

The smaller girl created a diversion by beginning to recite "On the Road to Mandalay". She only knew the first line, but she put her limited knowledge to the fullest possible use. She repeated the line over and over again in a dreamy but resolute and very audible voice; it seemed to the bachelor as though someone had had a bet with her that she could not carry on repeating the line aloud two thousand times without stopping. Whoever it was who had made the wager was likely to lose his bet.

"Come over here and listen to a story," said the aunt, when the bachelor had looked twice at her and once at the communication cord. The children moved listlessly towards the aunt's end of the carriage. Evidently her reputation as a story-teller did not rank high in their estimation.

In a low confidential voice, interrupted at frequent intervals by loud, petulant questions from her listeners, she began an unenterprising and deplorably uninteresting story about a girl who was good, and made friends with everyone on account of her goodness, and was finally saved from a mad bull by a number of rescuers who had admired her moral character.

"Wouldn't they have saved her if she hadn't been good?" demanded the bigger of the two girls. It was exactly the question that the bachelor had wanted to ask.

"Well, yes," admitted the aunt lamely, "but I don't think they would have run quite so fast to help her if they had not liked her so much."

"It's the stupidest story I've ever heard," said the bigger of the two girls, with immense conviction.

"I didn't listen after the first bit it was so stupid," said Cyril.

Theme 9: Writing for Children

The smaller girl made no actual comment on the story, but she had long ago recommenced a murmured repetition of her favourite line.

"You don't seem to be a success as a story-teller," said the bachelor suddenly from his corner.

The aunt bristled in instant defence at this unexpected attack.

"It's a very difficult thing to tell stories that children can both understand and appreciate," she said stiffly.

"I don't agree with you," said the bachelor.

"Perhaps you would like to tell them a story," was the aunt's retort.

"Tell us a story," demanded the bigger of the small girls.

"Once upon a time," began the bachelor, "there was a little girl called Bertha, who was extraordinarily good."

The children's momentarily aroused interest began at once to flicker; all stories seemed dreadfully alike, no matter who told them.

"She did all that she was told, she was always truthful, she kept her clothes clean, ate milk puddings as though they were jam tarts, learned her lessons perfectly, and was polite in her manners."

1 The bachelor goes on to tell a story which keeps the children entertained. Before you read any more, discuss in pairs what type of story the bachelor might have told.

"Was she pretty?" asked the bigger of the small girls.

"Not as pretty as any of you," said the bachelor, "but she was horribly good."

There was a wave of reaction in favour of the story; the word horrible in connection with goodness was a novelty that commended itself. It seemed to introduce a ring of truth that was absent from the aunt's tales of infant life.

"She was so good," continued the bachelor, "that she won several medals for goodness, which she always wore, pinned on to her dress. There was a medal for obedience, another medal for punctuality, and a third for good behaviour. They were large metal medals and they clinked against one another as she walked. No other child in the town where she lived had as many as three medals, so everybody knew that she must be an extra good child."

"Horribly good," quoted Cyril.

"Everybody talked about her goodness, and the Prince of the country got to hear about it, and he said that as she was so very good she might be allowed once a week to walk in his park, which was just outside the town. It was a beautiful park, and no children were ever allowed in it, so it was a great honour for Bertha to be allowed to go there."

"Were there any sheep in the park?" demanded Cyril.

"No," said the bachelor, "there were no sheep."

"Why weren't there any sheep?" came the inevitable question arising out of that answer.

The aunt permitted herself a smile, which might almost have been described as a grin.

"There were no sheep in the park," said the bachelor, "because the Prince's mother had once had a dream that her son would either be killed by a sheep or else by a clock falling on him. For that reason the Prince never kept a sheep in his park or a clock in his palace."

The aunt suppressed a gasp of admiration.

"Was the Prince killed by a sheep or by a clock?" asked Cyril.

"He's still alive, so we can't tell whether the dream will come true," said the bachelor unconcernedly; "anyway, there were no sheep in the park, but there were lots of little pigs running all over the place."

"What colour were they?"

"Black with white faces, white with black spots, black all over, grey with white patches, and some were white all over."

The story-teller paused to let a full idea of the park's treasures sink into the children's imaginations; then he resumed:

"Bertha was rather sorry to find that there were no flowers in the park. She had promised her aunts, with tears in her eyes, that she would not pick any of

The Story Teller.

the kind Prince's flowers, and she had meant to keep her promise, so of course it made her feel silly to find that there were no flowers to pick."

"Why weren't there any flowers?"

"Because the pigs had eaten them all," said the bachelor promptly. "The gardeners had told the Prince that you couldn't have pigs and flowers, so he decided to have pigs and no flowers."

There was a murmur of approval at the excellence of the Prince's decision; so many people would have decided the other way.

"There were lots of other delightful things in the park. There were ponds with gold and blue and green fish in them, and trees with beautiful parrots that said clever things at a moment's notice, and humming birds that hummed all the popular tunes of the day. Bertha walked up and down and enjoyed herself immensely, and thought to herself: 'If I were not so extraordinarily good I should not have been able to come into this beautiful park and enjoy all that there is to be seen in it,' and her three medals clinked against one another as she walked and helped to remind her of how very good she really was. Just then an enormous wolf came prowling into the park to see if it could catch a fat little pig for supper."

"What colour was it?" asked the children, amid an immediate quickening of interest.

"Mud-colour all over, with a black tongue and pale grey eyes that gleamed with unspeakable ferocity. The first thing that it saw in the park was Bertha; her pinafore was so spotlessly white and clean that it could be seen from a great distance. Bertha saw the wolf and saw that it was stealing towards her, and she began to wish that she had never been allowed to come to the park. She ran as hard as she could, and the wolf came after her in huge leaps and bounds. She managed to reach a shrubbery of myrtle bushes and she hid herself in one of the thickest of bushes. The wolf came sniffing among the branches, its black tongue lolling out of its mouth and its pale grey eyes glaring with rage. Bertha was terribly frightened, and thought to herself: 'If I had not been so good I should have been safe in the town at this moment.' However the scent of the myrtle was so strong that the wolf could not sniff out where Bertha was hiding, and the bushes were so thick that he might have hunted around in them for a long time without catching sight of her, so he thought he might as well go off and catch a little pig instead. Bertha was trembling very much at having the wolf prowling and sniffing so near her, and as she trembled the medal for obedience clinked against the medals for good conduct and punctuality. The wolf was just moving away when he heard the sound of the medals clinking and stopped to listen; they clinked again in a bush quite near him. He dashed into the bush, his pale green eyes gleaming with ferocity and triumph and dragged Bertha out and devoured her to the last morsel. All that was left of her were her shoes, bits of clothing, and the three medals for goodness."

"Were any of the little pigs killed?"

"No. They all escaped."

"The story began badly," said the smaller of the small girls, "but it had a beautiful ending."

"It is the most beautiful story that I have ever heard," said the bigger of the small girls, with immense decision.

"It is the only beautiful story that I have ever heard," said Cyril.

A dissentient opinion came from the aunt.

"A most improper story to tell to young children! You have undermined the effect of years of careful teaching."

"At any rate," said the bachelor, collecting his belongings preparatory to leaving the carriage, "I kept them quiet for ten minutes, which was more than you were able to do."

"Unhappy woman!" he observed to himself as he walked down the platform of Templecombe station; "for the next six months or so those children will assail her in public with demands for an improper story!"

Theme 9: Writing for Children

Imagine that you are the author of *The Story Teller* and you have sent it to a publisher. This is the reply you received.

> Dear Mr Barker,
>
> Re: The Storyteller
>
> Thank you for sending us your short story "The Storyteller". We think it would be suitable for publication in a forthcoming anthology but we have one or two suggested alterations to make which we think would improve it. We offer them for your consideration.
>
> (a) We suggest that the first paragraph should read as follows: "A woman was travelling by train with her two nieces and nephew. Occupying the same compartment was a bachelor." This conveys all the necessary information and would save space.
>
> (b) In the first part of the story you write, "The frown on the bachelor's face was deepening to a scowl. He was a hard, unsympathetic man, the aunt decided in her mind." We would like to omit those sentences. It is clear later in the story that the bachelor is not like this so the detail is confusing to the reader.
>
> (c) We would like to omit the unnecessary sentence which describes the man looking at the communication cord. This adds little to the story.
>
> (d) The success of the story depends on the contrast between the stories told by the aunt and bachelor but as they stand they are perhaps not different enough. Why do they have to both be about a girl who is "good"? Could they be altered?
>
> (e) The interruptions made by the children to the story told by the bachelor do not help the flow and we suggest that they be omitted.
>
> We hope we have not included too many alterations and hope that you will be able to make these changes. As I explained we would like to publish the story and would be grateful if you would suggest ideas for three accompanying drawings with which we could brief our artist.
>
> We look forward to hearing from you.
>
> Yours sincerely
>
> Antoinette Higgins

Now try......

2 You have been asked to prepare a birthday party for 7 to 12-year-olds.
☆ Decide whether they are boys, girls or a mixture of both, and in groups write a plan for the party. Use the following headings: *place, times for different activities, games, food, special items to remember.*

1 Your job is to write a detailed letter back to the publisher explaining why you cannot accept their suggestions and giving reasons.

3 Describe what happens when the aunt returns the children to their home and tells their parents about the incident on the train.

9.3 Writing a Story.

1 Your task is to write a story (or stories) for young children. You will need to do a good deal of preparation and thinking before you start the main writing. Work through the following stages, to get some initial ideas.

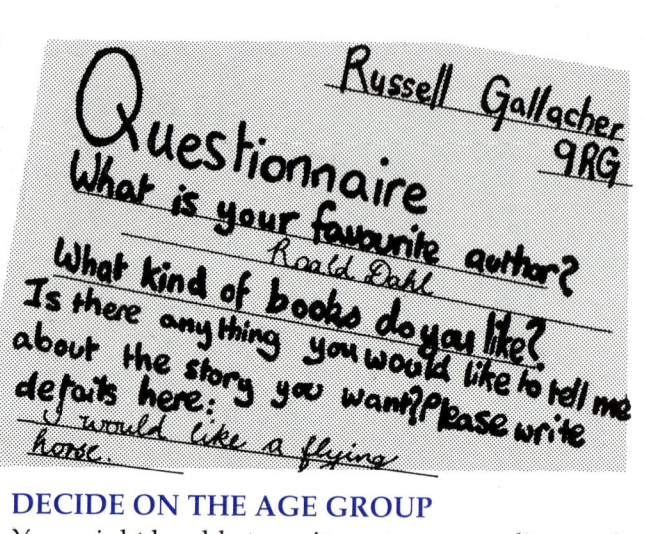

Questionnaire — Russell Gallacher 9RG
What is your favourite author? Roald Dahl
What kind of books do you like?
Is there anything you would like to tell me about the story you want? Please write details here: I would like a flying horse.

DECIDE ON THE AGE GROUP
You might be able to write a story according to the specifications of a young child :
- brother?
- sister?
- pupil in the local primary school?

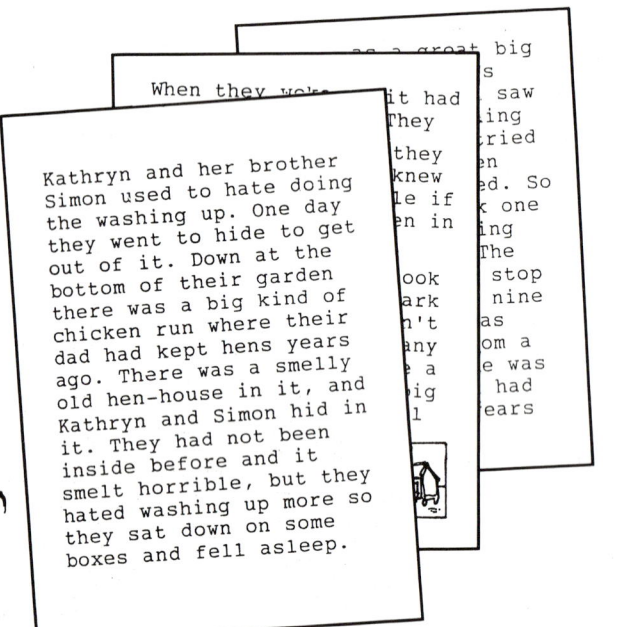

DECIDE ON THE TYPE OF BOOK
- Picture book?
- Pop up book?
- Story book mostly with text for slightly older pupils?
- Movable parts - figures which can be inserted, flaps which move?

Kathryn and her brother Simon used to hate doing the washing up. One day they went to hide to get out of it. Down at the bottom of their garden there was a big kind of chicken run where their dad had kept hens years ago. There was a smelly old hen-house in it, and Kathryn and Simon hid in it. They had not been inside before and it smelt horrible, but they hated washing up more so they sat down on some boxes and fell asleep.

DECIDE ON THE TYPE OF STORY AND CENTRAL CHARACTER
- Animals which talk?
- Fairy tale?
- Rhyming book?
- Naughty child?
- Everyday happenings, e.g. telling the time?
- Fantasy?
- Does your story have an educational purpose?

Theme 9: Writing for Children

PRODUCE A ROUGH DESIGN
- Number of pages?
- Type of pictures?
- Size of type?

PRACTISE READING THE FINISHED PRODUCT
Points to note:
- look up to keep children's attention.
- make sure they have a chance to see any illustrations.
- read at an appropriate speed.
- help them to understand by giving the right emphasis.

TRY IT OUT

Now try . . . . . .

2 Write a report of the whole project:
  ✔ the planning stages
  ✔ any pilot stages
  ✔ reaction of children when it was read to them.

75

10.1 On the Road.

In this unit you will be considering how a subject like that of "down and outs" can be presented in different ways both in literature and in the media.

The tramp is sometimes depicted in a way which suggests that the life is a pleasant one, travelling from town to town, not a care in the world. At other times sleeping rough is depicted as a cruel, hard, dangerous way of life. One could be described as a "romanticised" view whereas the other is a "realistic" view. If you complete the following table, adding some ideas of your own, it will help you to understand what those two terms mean.

The Romantic View	The Reality
Sleeping under the stars at night. Waking up to the sweet sound of birds singing. Travelling from town to town meeting interesting people on the way. Enjoying a life full of adventure and excitement. Cooking over an open fire.	Sleeping in a cold doorway on hard concrete.

1. Develop the contrast between the two pictures, **A** and **B** in the following ways.
   - ✓ Use the character in A in a strip cartoon of your own.
   - ✓ Include direct speech in bubbles as well as a commentary.
   - ✓ Write a list of random phrases and sentences which give a clue as to the life story of the character in B.
   - ✓ These could be direct speech (of friends, teachers, parents), thoughts, or comments by other people, e.g.
   "If you do that again Fred you'll be in trouble."
   "I'm sorry to bring you this bad news Mr. Smail."

2. Write the life story of the down and out in B to give an indication of the factors which brought him to this state. This could be a fairly brief summary or a major project giving considerable detail of different stages in his life. Either way, plan your work first.

Theme 10: On the Road

The following descriptions give brief glimpses of life on the road.

A

Paddy was my mate for about the next fortnight, and, as he was the first tramp I had known at all well, I want to give an account of him. I believe that he was a typical tramp and there are tens of thousands in England like him.

He was a tallish man, aged about thirty-five, with fair hair going grizzled and watery blue eyes. His features were good, but his cheeks had lanked and had that greyish, dirty in the grain look that comes of a bread and margarine diet. He was dressed rather better than most tramps, in a tweed shooting-jacket and a pair of old evening trousers with the braid still on them. Evidently the braid figured in his mind as a lingering scrap of respectability, and he took care to sew it on again when it came loose. He was careful of his appearance altogether, and carried a razor and bootbrush that he would not sell, though he had sold his 'papers' and even his pocket-knife long since. Nevertheless, one would have known him for a tramp a hundred yards away. There was something in his drifting style of walk, and the way he had of hunching his shoulders forward, essentially abject. Seeing him walk, you felt instinctively that he would sooner take a blow than give one.

George Orwell

B

The city had grown quiet at midnight and the moon was as white as early snow. A few cars moved slowly on Pearl Street but otherwise the streets were silent. Francis turned up his suitcoat collar and shoved his hands into his pants pockets. Alongside the mission the moon illuminated Sandra, who sat where they had left her. They stopped to look at her condition. Francis squatted and shook her.

"You sobered up yet, lady?"

Sandra answered him with an enveloping silence. Francis pushed the cowl off her face and in the vivid moonlight saw the toothmarks on her nose and cheek and chin. He shook his head to clear the vision, then saw that one of her fingers and the flesh between forefinger and thumb on her left hand had been chewed.

"The dogs got her." He looked across the street and saw a red-eyed mongrel waiting in the half-lit corner of an alley and he charged after it, picking up a stone as he went. The cur fled down the alley as Francis turned his ankle on a raised sidewalk brick and sprawled on the pavement.

He picked himself up, he now bloodied too by the cur, and sucked the dirt out of the cuts.

As he crossed the street, goblins came up from Broadway, ragged and masked, and danced around Helen. Pee Wee, bending over Sandra, straightened up as the goblin dance gained in ferocity.

"Jam and jelly, big fat belly," the goblins yelled at Helen. And when she drew herself inward they only intensified the chant.

"Hey you kids," Francis yelled. "Let her alone."

But they danced on and a skull goblin poked Helen in the stomach with a stick. As she swung at the skull with her hand, another goblin grabbed her purse and then all scattered.

William Kennedy

3 Both passages give very different views of what a tramp's life might be like.
Passage A gives a physical description of the tramp, whereas passage B uses two small incidents to convey something of what life is like.
- Say which passage you prefer and give some reasons for your preference.

4 Passage B gives a very grim view of life as a down and out. Even an incident as serious as this could be given a much lighter tone if written in a different way. E.g. "Hey that dog's been nibbling at Sandra..." Rewrite the passage trying to make it light and humorous and compare the two versions.

Now try . . . . . .

5 Imagine you are a film director and you need an actor to play the part of Paddy in passage A.
- Make notes on the kind of actor you are looking for and work out a brief exchange of dialogue and incident for the actor to perform as a screen test (a brief piece of film to show how well the actor will play the part).
- Ask different people to perform the extract.

10.2 Homeless.

For years people have lived rough. The tramp has been a traditional part of life in England. In recent years, however, more and more young people have been forced to sleep rough, particularly in large cities.

HOMELESS TEENAGERS MAY FACE JAIL

In the 1820s a Vagrancy Act was brought in to deal with vagabonds who were living rough. The legislation meant that anybody begging or living in the open could be prosecuted if complaints were received about them.

Now, over 100 years later, that same law exists and is being used to prosecute young teenagers who have been forced to live rough in our cities. The increase in the numbers of destitute young people is alarming but the use of this law as a solution to the problem is even more worrying.

We spoke to Susan and Jim, two 18 year olds who have been living rough for six months now. They told us that they have no choice but to ask people for money for food. They sleep in a variety of places (under bridges, in shop doorways) because they are constantly harassed by the police and public.

Homeless young people sleep rough alongside older tramps, drug addicts and alcoholics. They are forced to beg - to prosecute them and fine them is hardly likely to solve the problem. The law, which only seeks to hide the problem, should be repealed and a proper solution found.

---

1 This article is sympathetic to the plight of the teenagers and is presented in a non-sensational way. Rewrite the article with a different headline and style so that an unsympathetic view is given and the story is made more sensational and exaggerated.

2 Two teenagers are mentioned in the article. Work out a background for Susan and Jim by answering these questions:
- Where are they from?
- Why are they living rough?
- When did they meet?
- What are their hopes for the future?

3 Now, using the notes you have prepared as a basis, conduct an interview with one of the individuals as if for a radio documentary on living rough.
- ✓ This could be done in pairs or in larger groups, using a team to do the interviewing.
- ✓ The interviews could be performed for the rest of the class and a list made of the various issues which are raised.
- ✓ After each interview decide whether the interviewers were hostile or sympathetic to the teenagers living rough.

Theme 10: On the Road

In *The Runaway* by Ruth Thomas, Julia and Nathan are both loners and do not have any friends at school. They find some money and keep it, but when people start to ask questions they decide to run away. They meet in an old house late in the evening and then leave.

They left by the back door. Ahead of them, at the end of the tiny concreted yard, were iron railings topped with sharp spikes. Beyond was the railway embankment, and in a deep cutting there were tracks where trains chugged or thundered past at intervals.

"We'll get on the line," said Nathan. "No one won't see us there."

"Over the fence?"

"Course."

"I can't climb that."

"It's easy." Lithe as one of his cats, Nathan sprang at the rails and vaulted the spikes. "Come on."

"I can't."

"Come on. Someone'll catch us if you don't hurry up. They'll be looking for us any minute."

"They won't be looking for me. They think I'm asleep in bed."

"Well they'll be looking for me. Besides, we aren't allowed to be on the railway line."

Julia looked for something to stand on. A tub which had once held flowers raised her high enough so that she could lift one leg, fearfully, over the railings. "Hold my foot," she told Nathan. She threw the plastic bag on to the embankment, and grasped the railing with both hands.

"Jump now," said Nathan. He could see she wasn't going to make it, but there was no alternative. Julia lurched clumsily, and her foot caught Nathan square in the face as they both crashed to the ground. There was the sickening sound of cloth ripping as Julia's skirt tore on the spiked railing. Nathan's glasses were kicked off, and Julia sat on them as she fell. Neither child was hurt, but the back of Julia's skirt had a long jagged tear and Nathan's glasses, when they found them, were cracked right across on one side. It was a bad start.

Julia stood up to inspect the damage to her skirt.

"Get down," Nathan hissed.

Julia sat in the long grass.

"Right down," Nathan insisted.

"You said no one wouldn't see us here."

"They will if we stand up. We got to keep down in the grass. We got to crawl."

They crawled on their stomachs, the long summer grass waving around them. Anyone looking out of the windows of the houses opposite could have seen them quite easily, but there was at least the illusion of cover. It was uncomfortable going. The ground was soft from the recent rain, but there were hard stones under the grass which were rough on knees and elbows. Julia felt her knees being rubbed raw. She didn't think she wanted much more of this.

"How much further, Nathan?" she whimpered.

"Not far. There's an opening on to the road soon."

"But where we going after that?"

Nathan had no idea. "I dunno. Somewhere. A long way."

"Are we really running away, Nathan?" She couldn't wholly believe it, even now.

"Course we are, stupid."

A train pounded deafeningly past, only a metre or two from where they crawled.

"Where's this train going to?" asked Julia, who hardly ever went anywhere.

"Euston, I think," said Nathan, who had sometimes crossed London, visiting other members of his family.

"Shall we go to Euston then? On the train?"

"All right."

It was as good a suggestion as any.

They reached the gate which led to the pavement. Nathan raised his head and looked carefully round, peering as well as he could through one cracked lens and one whole one.

"Now!" he said, delivering the command in a theatrical hiss.

They bolted through the opening, which was ankle deep in litter. There were a few people on the pavement outside, but no one took the slightest notice of the children. They were used to kids playing illegally on the railway line, and anyway it was none of their business. The children were, of course, open to being spotted by any of Nathan's sisters who might have been sent out to look for him, but the risk was small as it was only a short step from here to the station.

When Nathan thought about his sisters he thought about his mum too - and then he made himself not think about his mum. He felt bad thinking about his mum. He even felt a little bit bad thinking about his dad. It made no difference though - he had to go, he had to.

"I'll get the tickets," said Julia, "and you just hide. We don't want the ticket man to see us together, he'll think it's funny."

Nathan loitered outside the station, while Julia

Homeless.

went inside.

"Two tickets to Euston," she said to the man in the little office.

"Halves?" said the man.

"Oh yes, halves," said Julia.

"Returns or singles?"

"What?"

"Are you coming back?"

"No," said Julia. "Singles please."

She'd forgotten about halves and singles. She'd almost slipped up there. She had a story ready about her sister, who was just coming to join her on the journey into Euston - but the ticket man was not interested. He was not even interested in the twenty pound note. Julia had another story to cover her possession of the twenty pound note, but no one wanted to hear it. The ticket man handed over the two tickets and the change, without comment.

Julia went outside to give Nathan his ticket, and the two passed separately through the barrier and down the steps to the platform. The train came soon, and they joined the other passengers in the big, yellow-panelled carriage with the green and brown seats. No one challenged them, no one noticed them particularly. Even the cracked glasses and torn skirt attracted no attention, it seemed. Now they were really on their way, it was all being almost too easy. "Are we really running away, Nathan?" Julia asked again.

"Yes!"

It was true. It was really happening. Julia's knees felt weak; she was glad she was sitting down.

"Are we nearly there?" Julia asked.

"Shut up," said Nathan scowling. "What you keep asking that for?"

The train slowed down and they saw it: EUSTON, in big letters. "What does that say?" asked Julia.

"Can't you read?" said Nathan, forgetting that indeed, she could not.

Julia blushed and turned her head.

The station was quite different from the friendly sunlit one they had started from. This station was covered over, dark and gloomy and somehow forbidding. The children showed their tickets at the barrier, and walked up the long ramp to the entrance. The vast marble hall that they found themselves in amazed them - even Nathan, who had seen it before but had forgotten how big it was. There was an appetizing smell of frying food coming from somewhere.

"I'm hungry," said Nathan, who had had nothing to eat since lunchtime, and Julia discovered that she was hungry too. They located a beefburger booth, one of the several places in the station selling cooked food. They bought beefburgers and cans of Coke and looked for somewhere to sit down. There were very few seats, so they sat on the floor.

They ate ravenously, in silence. "I'm going to have another one," said Nathan. He was enjoying the fun of having unlimited funds. You could have two beefburgers if you liked - three if you wanted them. Julia bought two bars of chocolate instead of another beefburger. She felt a little sick after she had gulped them down, but she was beginning to enjoy herself. Running away was all right, she decided, though there was still a nasty sinking frightened feeling, somewhere in the depths of her stomach, nothing to do with the chocolate, when she remembered what an awful thing they were doing.

There were other people sitting on the floor besides Julia and Nathan. Some of them looked rather peculiar. "They been drinking too much beer," said Nathan, disapprovingly.

Those who had been drinking too much beer took no notice of Julia and Nathan. But one or two other people were beginning to give them funny looks.

"Let's go now," said Julia. "Somebody might ask what we're here for."

"All right. I'm tired now anyway."

"Where we going to sleep?"

"Dunno. Somewhere."

Until that moment it had not really registered in either of their minds that they had no bed for the night. They contemplated the harsh reality with some misgivings.

"Perhaps there's another empty house," said Nathan, hopefully.

"Let's look," said Julia.

Outside the station it was beginning to get dark. There were no houses, empty or otherwise, only high brick walls and, on the other side of the road, the green paling surrounding a huge building site. The cranes inside the building site towered over the top of the paling.

"Shall we see if we can get in there?" said Julia.

They crossed the road and walked around the building site, trying to find a way in. Through the little cracks they could see that part, at least, of the area inside was roofed over. The floor looked dirty and hard, but at least there was a shelter. "There must be some way in," said Julia, reasonably. "The builders got to get in haven't they!"

Suddenly they came to a little space. Not very wide, just big enough for them to slip through one at a time. There was a woman walking her dog, but no one else in sight. Julia and Nathan walked on slowly

Theme 10: On the Road

past the opening until the woman had passed. Then they doubled back quickly, and dived through. "We made it," said Nathan, grinning for the first time that evening.

They chose a pillar to lie behind, and cleared a space of rubble. They couldn't clear away quite all the lumps, and the hard floor was dismayingly cold. Julia's sharp eyes spotted a pile of old sacks in a far corner. She went across and fetched two, to make some sort of bed.

"What about me?" said Nathan.

"You can get your own," said Julia. "I'm not your slave."

The sacks were very dirty, but it was better than freezing.

The children wriggled in them, trying to get comfortable.

"I don't like it here," said Julia, after a while. "It's spooky. I can't go to sleep."

"Shut up," said Nathan, sourly.

"No, I shan't shut up," said Julia. "I don't like Euston. And I don't like running away. I thought I did but I don't now. It's all horrible and scary....What was that?"

There was a noise that could have been footsteps over towards the opening into the building site. Terrified, Julia clutched at Nathan.

"Keep still," whispered Nathan, but he was scared too.

"Somebody's coming! Oh Nathan, I don't like it. Let's run, let's run!"

"Sh-sh-sh."

"It might be a robber come to steal my money."

"Sh-sh-sh, they gone now. I think they gone."

How could he be sure though? Nathan swallowed the lump of fear in his throat.

"I want to go home." said Julia in a small voice.

"We can't," said Nathan, suddenly wishing very much that they could.

"Yes we can. Why can't we? I don't care if my mum beats me. Anything's better than this."

"But we done it now. We run away didn't we. We made it worse. Whatever they was going to do to us before, they going to do worse now."

"What though? What can they do?"

"I dunno. Something bad though. Very bad."

"Oh Nathan, don't say that!"

"They going to be so angry though, I can't think about how angry they going to be, it makes me feel all funny in me belly."

Julia began to cry.

"No use crying. Come on, Ratbag, stop crying, that ain't going to help. Listen, we'll go somewhere else tomorrow. Somewhere good."

"Where is there good to go?"

Nathan considered. His fertile imagination had began to build a lovely, fantastic dream - but he wasn't ready to share that yet, and anyway it was only a dream. "Let's go to the seaside," he said. The seaside was part of his dream, but it had its own merits too.

"Oh yes," said Julia, forgetting some of her fright. "Let's do that Nathan."

The thought of going to the seaside was quite soothing. It distracted her mind from the eerie sounds, both real and imaginary, all around them. Distracted it too from the hardness of the ground and the dank odour of the sacks, and the smarting of her grazed knees. She slept a bit, and so did Nathan. The hours of darkness passed.

1 ☆ Using the information here and other ideas of your own prepare the school files which are kept on Julia and Nathan as part of the routine record keeping. These might contain: details of families, school reports, attendance, particular incidents at school, letters related to them.

2 The following situations could be either improvised or written out in script form.
- Nathan and Julia are approached by a policeman - what do they say?
- The family at home start to blame each other for what has happened.
- A scene which took place before the incident described here and which shows one reason why they are running away.

3 Continue the story of what happens when they arrive at the seaside. Plan your work around the way the two characters react differently to incidents or people they meet.

Now try . . . . . .

4 In groups prepare a radio documentary on the plight of young people living rough in cities. You could include:
- ✔ interviews with parents
- ✔ analysis of the causes
- ✔ interviews with runaways
- ✔ reports about where they sleep, eat, etc.

11.1 Manipulating Language.

In this unit you will be looking at how language can be manipulated to influence the way people think.

A

1) Your newspaper editor has given you picture A and told you to write a paragraph about it with the following caption: *"Slum school conditions in which pupils and teachers have to work"*.
☆ Then he changed his mind. He told you to write a new paragraph to accompany the same picture, but with the following caption: *"This is how pupils treat their schools"*.
What can you say about the choice of words in each case?

Newspapers create powerful images in the minds of their readers by combining pictures and captions.

B

2) Look at picture B, and write two captions both of which COULD be used with it, but which would give very different impressions.

3) Write a sentence describing a possible newspaper picture and write 2 captions for it, one favourable and one unfavourable.

Now try . . . . . .

4) Collect pictures from newspapers which have captions that are either favourable or unfavourable.
- Write your own captions to give an opposite impression from that of the original.
- Was it easy to find examples of pictures being "used" by newspapers in this way?

Theme 11: Manipulating Language

☆ **DOUBLESPEAK**

Organisations which need to communicate with the general public are sometimes guilty of deliberately misusing the language to give false impressions. A group of people in the United States of America were so concerned by this that they came together to discourage "Doublespeak" as they called it. They describe Doublespeak as follows:

"Doublespeak is language used to lie or mislead while pretending to tell the truth. Doublespeak is widespread and increasing. It is used by the highest elected official, by bureaucrats in state and local government, by members of industry, academia, and other areas of society in order to deceive, to make the bad seem good, the negative appear positive, the disastrous seem tolerable. Doublespeak misleads about issues vital to people's health, their prosperity, even their very lives."

An example is when a company advertising health insurance referred to death as "terminal living" because they wanted to sell their insurance to people rather than frighten them off by using a direct word.

5 In the lefthand column of table C, are examples of Doublespeak taken from real life. In the righthand column are their actual meanings. Match up the Doublespeak expression with its correct meaning.

C

DOUBLESPEAK	ACTUAL
1. interact with print	A Secondhand car dealer
2. chronologically gifted	B cows, pigs, chickens
3. inhalation hazard	C unconscious
4. action toys	D budget cuts
5. purchase adviser of previously distinguished automobiles	E boys' dolls
	F salesperson
6. energy documents	G read
7. pavement deficiencies	H poison gas
8. secure facility	I old people
9. grain-consuming animal units	J jail
10. non-decision-making state	K electricity bill
11. advanced downward adjustments	L pot holes
12. marketing consultant	

Speech bubble in illustration: COGNISANCE OF THE MATTER-LACKING-LOCATION TERRESTRIAL-MASS-REMOVAL INSTRUMENT IS A COMMUNAL ACCOUTREMENT.

Now try . . . . . .

6 Choose six pairs from the table and suggest what organisations or people might have used the Doublespeak and why.

83

11.2 Say What You Mean!

In 1990 an article appeared in a Sunday newspaper about "Doublespeak". It was written by William Lutz and the following is an abridged version.

HOW NOT TO SAY WHAT YOU MEAN IF YOU DON'T MEAN WHAT YOU SAY.

Aircraft don't crash; they have "uncontrolled contact with the ground".

Doublespeak continues to spread as the official language of public discourse. It is a language which avoids, shifts or denies responsibility, a language at variance with its real meaning.

When shopping, we are asked to check our packages at the till "for our convenience". It's not for our convenience at all, but for the store's "programme to reduce inventory shrinkage". We see advertisements for "preowned", "experienced" or "previously distinguished" cars; for "genuine imitation leather", or "real counterfeit diamonds".

We know that a toothbrush is still a toothbrush even if the advertisements on television call it a "home plaque removal instrument"; we also know that "nutritional avoidance therapy" means a diet. But who would guess that "volume-related production schedule adjustment" means closing a factory? Or that "energetic disassembly" means an explosion in a nuclear power plant?

In 1984 (sic) the U.S. State Department announced that in annual reports on international human rights it would no longer use the word "killing". Instead it chose the phrase "unlawful or arbitrary deprivation of life". The State Department thus avoided discussing government-sanctioned murders in countries America supports.

In 1979, a National Airlines 727 crashed while trying to land at Pensacol airport in Florida, killing three passengers and injuring 21. Since the insured value of the plane was greater than its book value, National made an insurance profit of 1.7 million dollars. In its annual report, National said that the profit was due to "the involuntary conversion of a 727".

Military doublespeak has its own terminology. The invasion of Grenada was conducted not by the U.S. Army, Navy, Air Force and Marines, but by "Caribbean peace-keeping forces". But then, according to the Pentagon, it wasn't an invasion at all - it was a "pre-dawn vertical insertion".

Doublespeak is not the product of careless language or sloppy thinking. On the contrary, serious doublespeak is carefully designed to appear to communicate, but in fact to mislead.

It's not a Titan 11 nuclear-armed, intercontinental ballistic missile 630 times more powerful than the atomic bomb dropped on Hiroshima; it's just a "very large, potentially disruptive re-entry system", so don't worry about the threat of nuclear destruction.

Serious doublespeak breeds suspicion, distrust and, ultimately, hostility.

Theme 11: Manipulating Language

1. In pairs, choose six examples of *Doublespeak* from the passage.
   - In each case give the real meaning and then write notes explaining why the writer chose the original wording. Be as precise as you can.
   - Share your ideas as a class.

2. Do you think use of such language is ever justifiable? You might want to soften a particularly bad piece of news, for example.
   - Discuss in pairs and note down what you think and why.
   - Share your ideas as a class.

   MULTIPLE DUPLICATION BEHAVIOUR ORIENTATION EXPERIENCE.

   NORTH BEDLAM COMPREHENSIVE SCHOOL
   SITE SPECIFIC KNOWLEDGE BESTOWMENT ESTABLISHMENT.

3. Invent your own doublespeak! Manufacture doublespeak alternatives for the following:
   - I am hopeless at —— (put in your own choice of subject).
   - I have not done any of the work.
   - I have failed my examination.
   - The teacher lost his/her temper with me.
   - I have been put in detention.
   - I have been suspended from school for 3 days.

4. Where do you think you will find examples of Doublespeak?
   - As a class, decide on a number of headings under which to search. Then start collecting.
   - Your aim is to make a class collection of originals - and translations in clear English.
   Work in the following ways:
   ✓ Decide on sections and headings.
   ✓ Appoint 2 people to be in charge of each section.
   ✓ Share out the tasks - i.e. who is going to concentrate on searching where. A collection of newspapers should give you masses to work on - in news stories, articles, advertisements of different kinds, and so on. But also keep your eyes and ears open. Look at notices, any reports of meetings, junk mail and the spoken word on radio or television.
   ✓ Write up your examples - originals and clear English translations - in the agreed format. Hand in to the appropriate section leaders.
   ✓ Put up the display.

   SUBJECT ORIENTATED ERUDITION TRANSMISSION SPECIALIST.

   ### Now try . . . . . .

5. Choose one of the sections and write an amusing article using the material. Mockery is a powerful form of criticism.

11.3 Word Associations.

Here are some different ways of manipulating language so that you can achieve the exact effect you are trying for.

SYNONYMS - words with the same meaning.

ANTONYMS - words with opposite meanings.

SCENT   STINK

SHORT   TALL

All words carry associations with them. Suppose you chose a particularly brightly coloured shirt and then two friends commented on it. One called it "brilliant" and the other called it "flash". You would understand who liked it and who did not.

A
Two people attended the same disco. One enjoyed it and the other hated it. They both described the experience afterwards, using exactly the same facts, as follows:
Disco - lots of people - lasted 6 hours - flashing lights - crowds at the bar - loud music - regular rhythms - danced energetically - tried to talk, but too noisy - exhausted at end.

1 Take the facts in **A** and tell the story twice, once for the person who enjoyed it and once for the one who didn't. In each case you could start off, "I went to a disco last night," but what for one was a strong, rhythmic beat, for the other might be a deafening, monotonous thudding.

If you are trying to sell something, choice of words with the right associations is essential.

B
This elegant resort has popular beaches of golden sand and colourful pebbles. The modern hotels are conveniently situated along the seafront and the contemporary shops tempt the tourist with wonderful shopping opportunities, especially for fashion, sportswear, gifts and hand-made confectionery. Nights are lively with American bars, cafes, night clubs and a casino.

C
This pretentious seaside town has crowded beaches of shingle, with a few sandy bits. Characterless hotels crowd together, spoiling the seafront, and the town centre contains mainly expensive shops selling luxury goods. It's difficult to get to sleep at night because of all the noisy nightlife.

These two descriptions in **B** and **C** describe the same resort, and refer to the same facts; all that is different is the attitude of the writer towards them, and therefore the choice of words.

Theme 11: Manipulating Language

D is a description of another holiday resort, such as might appear on a brochure.

> **D**
> This beautiful, historic town is a maze of picturesque, narrow streets lined by centuries-old, half-timbered houses; traffic is banned from them. There is a fascinating museum, unchanged for half a century, and a colourful fish quay with the distinctive scent of the sea harvest. The traditional hotels are full of character and the cafes serve the famous local dishes, specially prepared for tourists. You feel you are stepping back in time as you holiday in this corner of ....

2 Rewrite the description in D as if it were written by a disgruntled holiday maker who hated his or her stay there.

E *[cartoon of shops: THE WOOL BAA, A CUT ABOVE, VERS-A-TILE, NUT HOUSE, FRED'S PLAICE, SPECIALEYES]*

3 Now take wherever you live - not the entire town, city, or even village, but just your corner, perhaps a few streets. Write up its charms in a paragraph for a brochure. Your aim is to try to persuade the reader to visit there. Read out and vote for the most appealing descriptions.

4 ☆ Collect holiday brochures and compile a dictionary of words and phrases commonly used in their descriptions - with your rather cynical translations. List your finished product alphabetically.

5 Look at the cartoon in **E**. In pairs, write down as many examples of similar shop names as you can think of in ten minutes and then invent some new names of your own for shops or cafes.

We are continually adding new words to our language. Sometimes words become overused and lose their impact. New technology demands new words.

Now try . . . . . .

6 ☆ Try listing as many words as you can which have been recently added to the language.

7 ☆ In this Unit and in other parts of the book you have looked quite closely at ways in which language can be manipulated. You have been asked to write an article for a magazine on the subject of Manipulating Language.
This is not a subject which is obviously appealing, so you must present it in an interesting way:
✓ Choose a catchy title.
✓ Find an opening which makes the casual reader want to continue.
✓ Use a lively style.
✓ You may also decide to illustrate it.
✓ You also have the problem of knowing too much for your article, so you will have to select what material to use.

87

12.1 Own Reading.

In this unit you will be embarking on a project designed to extend your own wider reading according to your own preference.

It is sometimes interesting to base your reading of literature on different pieces of writing which are linked in some way.

Your choice of reading could be based on one of the following:

THEME
Here the poetry, plays, novels, stories are based on one particular subject. You could start with a choice of subject and look for appropriate reading, or you could base your theme on a story or poem and look for related works.

GENRE
The word "genre" means a category. In the case of literature it can just mean poetry, novels or plays. Alternatively it can refer to a more precise category like science fiction, romance, horror, westerns, etc.

AUTHOR
The works (either all novels, short stories, plays or poems or a mixture of genres) are written by one person. If you have read a story by an author which you enjoyed you may like to find out what else they have written. You may be surprised to find out they have written other types of literature.

COUNTRY
A project of this kind would need extra research but could be very interesting, particularly if you or your family originally come from a different country.

Theme 12: Own Reading

You will also need to decide how to present the results of your reading. Here are some suggestions:

READING LOG
This is a diary which you keep as you read giving your immediate reactions and responses. These may change as you read; the idea is not to change what you have written but to keep it as an ongoing record.

DISPLAY
A wall display or booklet with details of your reading, pictures and commentary might entice others to read some of the same material.

ORAL PRESENTATION
You will need to make some notes but the final product will be a presentation giving your opinions about the reading you have completed.

CREATIVE RESPONSES
A creative piece like your own similar story or poem can be an effective way of responding to your reading.

You should make a rough plan indicating the sort of project you might like to undertake. The work on the short story on page 90, *The Mysteries of the Heart* by Nigel Hinton, should give you some ideas and time to think before you make your final commitment.

89

12.2 The Mysteries of...

A short story like this one, *The Mysteries of the Heart* by Nigel Hinton, could be the starting point for your reading project.

"Come on Sherlock, do your detective stuff and find my cheque-book for me."

Alan's mum was always losing things and for as long as he could remember he had helped her find them. Sometimes they were silly little things like a pair of scissors or a kitchen knife but sometimes they were big things. Like the time they went on a day trip to France and she lost their passports. Everybody had gone rushing around the supermarket in a panic - even dad - but Alan had decided to run back to the cafe where they'd had lunch and he had found the passports under a table.

"How do you do it?" his mum always asked, smiling with relief, when he handed her something she had lost.

He really didn't know - he just got a feeling about where to look and most of the time he was right. His dad said it must be ESP but his younger sister, Janey, said it was because he was a busybody who liked poking his nose into everything. Of course, that didn't stop her asking him for help when she lost something but the funny thing was that he hardly ever managed to find things for her.

In fact it really only worked for his mum and that was probably because he hated it when she looked helpless or upset. Whenever he saw those worry lines crease up around her eyes there was a small stab in his heart and he just wanted to make everything all right for her. That was partly why he hadn't gone to breakfast this morning. His dad's friend had rung to ask if anyone wanted to go sailing with him in his new boat and his dad had said, "You bet. I'd love to come and so would Janey."

As soon as he put the phone down he sort of apologized to Alan, saying that there was only enough room for three in the boat and that Janey deserved a treat because she had been ill for a couple of weeks. That was true but Alan still felt it wasn't fair just to choose her without talking about it first. He'd started to say something but he'd seen those worry lines suddenly appear round his mum's eyes so he'd forced a smile and said it was OK. The worry lines had gone so it had been worth it. But now they were back again.

"What on earth could I have done with it?" his mum was saying as she searched through her bag looking for her cheque-book. "Come on Sherlock - do your trick. Dad'll do his nut if I can't find it."

"Don't be silly - dad never does his nut about anything. He just goes quiet."

"That's what I mean. He goes all quiet and understanding and I feel such a fool. That's because I am one, I suppose."

"You're not," Alan said, putting his arm round her shoulder and noticing that he was as tall as she was now.

"Well, let's just say that I make more mistakes than most people." She turned and looked him straight in the eyes.

"I'll be taller than you soon," he said. "Taller than dad, too. Fancy two shorties like you having a beanpole like me."

Her eyes flicked away from his for a moment then she laughed and said, "OK, Beanpole, can you see my cheque-book from your great height?"

"Don't worry, I'll find it," he said.

But he didn't. He kept thinking of places - down the side of the sofa; behind the fridge; under the kitchen table - but each time he was wrong.

"It's no good, love," his mum said, at last. "I've got to go - the shops close early on Saturdays. I'll get some money out of the machine at the bank."

She asked if he wanted to go with her but he said

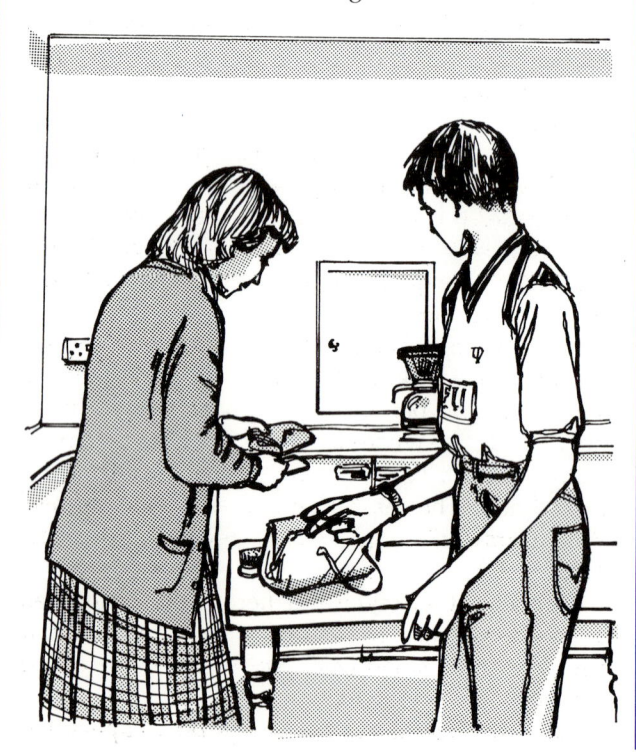

90

no - the cheque-book had to be somewhere in the house and he'd made up his mind he was going to find it. She grabbed a basket, put on a coat and rushed out of the house.

As soon as she'd gone he sat on the stairs and tried to concentrate: where was the cheque-book? After a moment he stood up and walked up the stairs to his parents' bedroom. He looked around the room casually and noticed that his dad had left the top off his bottle of aftershave. The bedroom always smelled strongly: a combination of his mum's perfume, his dad's aftershave and a vaguely dusty smell from the old pink carpet.

He picked up the aftershave, splashed some into his hand and then slapped it onto his face. He liked the smell of it and the slight sting on his skin. He looked in the mirror and couldn't help smiling at himself - it was silly putting on aftershave when he didn't shave yet. He peered closer: there was a definite fuzz round his chin and across his upper lip. It was strange to think that he was going to change - that he had already stopped being a boy and was getting ready to become a man.

In the mirror he saw the open door of his parents' wardrobe. He turned around and walked across to it. There, on the floor next to a pair of shoes, was the cheque-book. He picked it up and slipped it into his pocket. So, he was still the ace detective and he would be able to give his mum a surprise when she got home. He was about to turn away when he saw the small metal box at the back of the wardrobe, half-hidden by one of his mum's coats. He bent down and pulled it out.

It was locked.

Perhaps Janey was right - perhaps he was just a busybody - but suddenly he wanted to find out what was inside. It was a mystery and detectives always wanted to solve mysteries. Why was it locked? No, that wasn't the question yet. Where was the key? - that was the question.

He put the metal box on the bed and looked around the room. It was like that game where you hunted for something and people told you whether you were hot or cold. So - where was the key? The wardrobe? Cold. Ice cold. Nobody would leave the key near a locked box. The chest of drawers? Much warmer. Which drawer? Top? Cold. Second? Warmer. Third? Hot.

He opened the drawer and there, in the corner, was a little jewellery-box. He lifted the lid. Two rings, a necklace and a small key. Not bad. His detective instinct was working well.

He sat on the bed and opened the box. Papers. He flicked through them. Insurance policies, deeds to the house - official documents, that was all. Nothing interesting.

Then why was his heart beating so fast? Why was all his detective instinct telling him that there was something important here?

He unfolded one of the papers. It was his parents' marriage certificate. There was his dad's name: Leonard John Lewis, and his mum's name: Susan Eva Bumstead. Thank goodness she'd married someone with a better name. He could just imagine all the boring jokes he would have had to put up with if his name had been Bumstead.

He started to re-fold the certificate and then stopped when he saw the date on the bottom. He thought it must be a mistake but then he checked and saw that the same date was written in two other places. His chest tightened and a wave of heat swept up his neck to his face.

His mum and dad had only been married for ten years. They had got married two years after he was born.

It was a shock, but it wasn't terrible. It just made him want to giggle. Lots of people got married because they were going to have a baby. Some people didn't even bother to get married at all. Why had his mother and dad waited that long, though? Two whole years - nearly two and a half, actually. He did a quick calculation. That meant that his mum was already expecting Janey when they got married. They

The Mysteries of the Heart.

must have got married because of Janey. In that case, why hadn't they bothered to get ...?

Another wave of heat burned his face. He dropped the paper on the bed and began searching through the box. If there was a marriage certificate there were probably birth certificates, too. Yes. Here was Janey's. Date of birth - six months after the marriage. And this one must be his. He unfolded it.

The date of birth. The place of birth. His names. His mum's names. All the details. Except that under the column headed 'Name and Surname of Father' it didn't say Leonard John Lewis.

A shiver shook his whole body. His dad was not his dad.

After the shiver a great calm filled him. His mum might be home soon. He put the papers back, locked the box and returned it to the wardrobe, making sure it was just where he'd found it. Then he straightened the cover of the bed - his mum's and Leonard John Lewis' bed. Then he put the key back in the jewellery-box and closed the drawer.

He did it all calmly but it was as if the shiver had opened up his senses wider than they had ever been before. His eyes, ears, nose, taste-buds and skin were recording everything: the pressure of the air, the patterns of light on the carpet, the touch of his mum's coat on his skin as he put the box back. They were recording everything and he knew that he would remember this moment for the rest of his life.

Back in his own bedroom he lay on the bed and stared at the ceiling. It didn't hurt yet. It never did at first. When his dog had been killed by that lorry he hadn't cried or felt any pain until nearly two days after it happened.

He wouldn't say anything to them, not until the pain came. He wouldn't be able to bear those worry lines round his mum's eyes, or his dad's - Leonard John Lewis' - quietness, when he told them he knew. When the pain came it might be different. It might hurt so much that he would have to tell them. He wasn't as good at keeping things secret as they were.

Janey was right: he was a nosy busybody. Well, he'd paid for it this time. The ace detective had solved a mystery and he wished he hadn't. He wished he had gone on never knowing that there was a mystery. Although, thinking about it now, he could see all those millions of tiny clues over the years: the little looks, the sentences started but never finished, the sudden changes in mood. And the bigger clues of course: the way it had always felt like him and mum together and Janey and his... Janey and Leonard John Lewis together. No, a real detective would have spotted the truth years before. He was still only a boy detective and he realized how many mysteries he knew nothing about. How could you live with people and not know them? How could people keep secrets hidden in their hearts so long? And why? He had such a lot to learn. He would have to be more on his toes for the next case.

And, of course, the next case would be a real challenge - he would be trying to find a missing person. There weren't many clues; just the name on a birth certificate: Colin Mark Drake. Oh yes, there was one other detail to help a detective - there was a strong likelihood that this mysterious stranger was tall: certainly taller than Susan Eva Bumstead and Leonard John Lewis. See, he was getting better at this game already. He was learning to put two and two together.

Alan laughed and said out loud, "They don't call me Sherlock for nothing."

Then he turned and pressed his face into the pillow. The pain had come much earlier than he had expected. And with the pain came the tears.

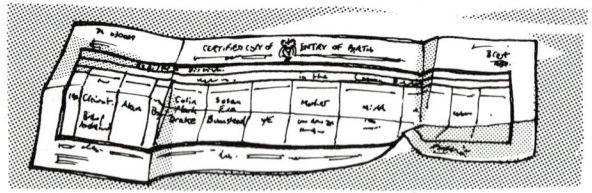

The following questions are designed to get you thinking more deeply about the story.

1. The story ends with the sentence, "And with the pain came the tears." Why did Alan feel so hurt?

2. When you read the story a second time there are clues about his family circumstances - how many of these can you find?

3. Were his parents right not to tell him the truth? At what age should children be told the truth in a situation like this?

4. What impression do you get of Alan?

5. "Mysteries of the Heart" is a complete short story in itself. If the author had decided to continue it, how might he have done so?

Theme 12: Own Reading

A creative response to the story can also provide an opportunity for the reader to show an understanding of the characters and themes. Here are some examples of creative assignments and ideas to help you choose which one to try.

1 Describe Alan's next meeting with his stepfather.

It is important that you keep the character of Alan in your writing consistent with that of the original. Is he the sort of person who would blurt out his discovery or would he keep it to himself, for a while at least? You might find that an effective way of dealing with the meeting is not to have the characters talk directly about what has happened. However at the end of the conversation the stepfather has a good idea that Alan knows.

2 Write out the conversation which took place between Alan's mother and his stepfather when they realise that Alan knows the truth.

Here you have an opportunity to show whether the mother and stepfather might have had different views about telling Alan the truth in the past. We are not really told this in the story. Does this new development put a strain on their relationship?

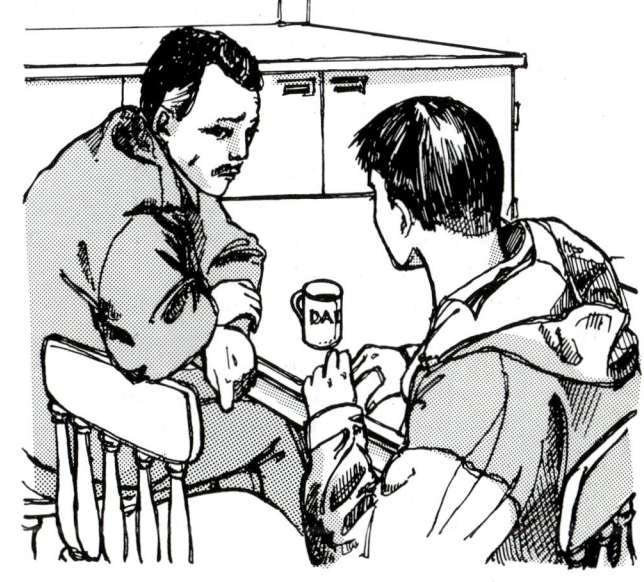

3 Write the letter which Alan received from his real father a week after the events in the story.

This is a difficult task for you because it is a difficult task for the father! Therefore, if your writing is a little awkward and if you are uncertain what to say, that might make the letter more realistic.

4 Rewrite the story in the form of a one-act play in which a friend of Alan's is with him when he makes the discovery.

You can use the conversation with the friend to convey important information which came at the start of the story. When the discovery is actually made it might be more effective to have Alan simply go quiet and ask to be alone rather than discuss the matter with a friend.

93

12.3 Starting Points.

The Mysteries of the Heart could be a part of a number of themes - as could almost any story you use as a starting point. If you choose a broad theme such as "Growing Up" for example, it will give you a considerable amount of scope for choosing other literature. You will find it useful to browse in the library, look through poetry anthologies and magazines such as **BOOKS FOR KEEPS**. You could also ask for suggestions from people. This unit also shows you how you can organise your research around authors and genres.

☆ **RESEARCH:** *BOOKS FOR KEEPS*

THEME: GROWING UP

DRAMA
Our Day Out - Willy Russell
Gregory's Girl - Gerald Cole
P'Tang, Yang, Kipperbang - Jack Rosenthal
Manjit - Lakviar Singh (Festival Plays - Longman)

NOVELS
Lord of the Flies - William Golding
The Country Girls - Edna O'Brien
It's My Life - Robert Leeson
Black Boy - Richard Wright
Joby - Stan Barstow
There Is a Happy Land - Keith Waterhouse
Badger on the Barge - Janni Hawker
Worlds Apart - Jill Murphy
Roll of Thunder, Hear My Cry - Mildred Taylor

POEMS
Bye Child - Seamus Heaney
Prayer Before Birth - Louis MacNeice
First Death - D J Enright
What Has Happened to Lulu - Charles Causley

SHORT STORIES
The Lumber Room - Saki
Flight - Doris Lessing
Growing Up - Joyce Cary
My Oedipus Complex - Frank O'Connor
The Opposite Sex - Laurie Lee

Theme 12: Own Reading

☆ **AUTHOR: MAYA ANGELOU**

Maya Angelou is one of the world's best-selling black authors. She is now a professor of American literature at an American University, but her amazingly varied career and the experience of being a black woman has become the subject matter of her work.

Born in 1928, in St Louis Missouri, she was raped at the age of 8 by her mother's boyfriend and for 5 years after became mute. At 16 she gave birth to a son, and in the years following her graduation was a waitress, dancer, professional singer (she toured Europe in the important production of the opera Porgy and Bess), editor for a newspaper in Ghana, friend and colleague of Martin Luther King, active in the Black Rights movement and a founder member of the Harlem Writer's Guild.

Autobiographical works:

I Know Why the Caged Bird Sings
Gather Together in My Name
Singin' and Swingin' and
Gettin' Merry Like Christmas
The Heart of a Woman
All God's Children Need Travelling Shoes

Poetry:

And Still I rise
Just Give Me a Cool Drink of Water 'Fore I Die
Now Sheba Sings the Song

GENRE: *Romance*

NOVELS AND SHORT STORIES
Beautiful Losers - Barbara Weston
The Basketball Game - J. Lester
Love All - compiled by A. Chambers
It Must Be Different - compiled by Bryan Newton
Sumitra's Story - Rukshana Smith
Try some Mills and Boon novels for a contrast!

PLAYS
Love Is a Many Splendoured Thing - Alan Bleasdale
Still Waters and Other Plays - Julia Jones
Some Enchanted Evening - Cecil Taylor
Wrong First Time - Peter Terson

POEMS
First Ice - Andrew Vaznesensky
Where Shall We Go - Vernon Scannell
Several poems in the Anthology
"Axed Between the Ears"
edited by David Kitchen.

Now try . . . . . .

1 ☆ You should now develop your own reading list and produce your reading project. You should form an initial list of reading material and an idea of how you are going to present the final outcome before you embark on your reading.

Acknowledgements.

The Publishers would like to thank the following authors and publishers for permission to reproduce their material:

The Ice Cart by W.W. Gibson - Macmillan London and Basingstoke.

The Nightmare extract taken from Chinese Poems translated by Arthur Waley reproduced by kind permission of Unwin Hyman Ltd.

Enough Is Too Much Already from Feet and Other Stories by Jan Mark (Kestrel Books 1983), © Jan Mark 1983.

The Guardian Newspaper

Fawlty Towers © John Cleese and Connie Booth - David Wilkinson Associates.

Extract from *Regulation 2* of the Control of Misleading Advertisements Regulations, 1988.

Advertising Standards Authority Limited.

Extract from *Alice in Genderland* by permission of Pat Barrett and the NCC.

The Flute Player by Ruskin Bond from Taking Root by Anthony Masters - Octopus Publishing Group.

A Kind of Loving by Stan Barstow published by Michael Joseph Ltd. © 1960 by Stan Barstow.

Fog from Chicago Poems © 1916 by Holt, Rinehart & Winston, Inc. and renewed 1944 by Carl Sandburg reprinted by permission of Harcourt Brace Jovanovich, Inc.

A Local Train of Thought by Siegfried Sassoon by permission of George Sassoon.

Extract from *The Only Child* by James Kirkup © author 1957. Reproduced by permission of Curtis Brown Ltd. on behalf of the author.

Extract from *A Prospect of the Sea* by Dylan Thomas - the Trustees for the © of Dylan Thomas.

Extract from *Cider with Rosie* by Laurie Lee - The Hogarth Press.

Extract from *How Many Miles to Babylon* by Jennifer Johnson - Hamish Hamilton Ltd.

The Miser from My Oedipus Complex and Other Stories by Frank O'Connor reprinted by permission of the Peters Fraser & Dunlop Group Ltd.

Extracts from *Clinging to the Wreckage* by John Mortimer & *Under the Eye of the Clock* by Christopher Nolan by permission of George Weidenfeld & Nicolson Ltd.

Extract from *Timebends* by Arthur Miller - Methuen Publishers.

Extract from *Roots* by Alex Haley, Random Century Group, Hutchinson Publishers.

Yok - Yok The Frog © 1978 by Anne van der Essen and Etienne Delessert.

Not Now Bernard by David McKee by permission of Anderson Press.

The Story Teller by Saki - The Bodley Head.

Extract from *Down and Out in London and Paris* by George Orwell. Estate of the late Sonia Brownell Orwell and Secker & Warburg.

Extract from *Ironweed* by William Kennedy (Penguin Books, 1984) © William Kennedy 1979, 1981, 1983.

Runaways by Ruth Thomas - the author and Hutchinson Children's Books.

Mysteries of the Heart by Nigel Hinton © Nigel Hinton 1989.

Books For Keeps, 6 Brightfield Road, Lee, London SE12 8QF.

PHOTOGRAPHS

The publishers would like to acknowledge:
p76 Salvation Army
p78 Salvation Army
p82 Terry Brown
p95 Virago Press

ILLUSTRATORS

Eric Jones, Phillip Hogson, Paul Bevan.
Cover design by Tanglewood Graphics, Broadway House, The Broadway, London SW19. Tel: 071 543 3048.
Cover illustration by Abacus Publicity Ltd.

The publishers have made every effort to contact copyright holders but this has not always been possible. If any have been overlooked we will be pleased to make any necessary arrangements.

ANSWERS

Page 28

A = 'Barry, how often do I have to tell you not to lick your plate!'

B = 'You don't accept sheep! What kind of planet is this?'